THE MIDDLE WAY LEADER

Strategic thinking for managing people, processes, and profit

PAM NURRIE

To my parents, Patricia and Eugene,
who taught me the power of hard work and positive thinking.

And my children, Clayton and Cass, who color my world and
continue to inspire me.

TABLE OF CONTENTS

Dedication   v

Introduction   **xiii**

   Mess to Success   xiv

   The Entrepreneur's Life   xviii

   Business Assessment Form   xxiv

PART ONE: MAKE FINANCIALS YOUR SUPERPOWER   **3**

Chapter 1: Cash   **5**

   Profit and Loss   6

   Revenue   9

   Revenue Evaluation   9

   Earnings Multiple   10

   Cost of Goods Sold   10

   Overhead   11

   Increasing Revenue   11

   Reducing COGS   12

   Reducing Overhead   13

   The Magic Formula   14

Chapter 2: Capital   **17**

   Top-Line Growth   18

   Increase Price or Cut Costs   19

   Sell More Stuff   20

   Sales Playbook   21

   Pump Up the Volume   23

   Upsell, Cross-sell, and Down-sell 24

   Accounts Receivable   25

Chapter 3: COGS   27

    Pricing   27

    Discounting   28

    Too Much Inventory   30

    Supplier Price Increase   30

    On-Demand Manufacturing   31

    Bundle to Eliminate Waste   32

    Improve Quality Control   32

    Drop-Shipping   33

Chapter 4: Costs   35

    Cutting versus Slashing   36

    Credit Card Expenses   37

    Negotiate with Vendors and Suppliers   37

    Know Your Marketing ROI   38

Chapter 5: Capacity   41

    Invest in Culture, Reduce Turnover   42

    Automation Versus Outsourcing   42

    Tap into the Gig Economy   43

    Goals and Priorities   44

    Conduct a Productivity Review   44

    Invest in a Strategic Partner   45

Chapter 6: Crystal Balls   47

    Benchmarking   48

    Forecasting   48

    Seasonality   49

    Pro Forma   49

    Profitability   50

    Three Buckets   51

PART TWO: CARVE A MIDDLE WAY PATH TO   LEADERSHIP MASTERY   55

Chapter 7: Twelve Principles   57

    The Middle Way   57

    The Twelve Principles of Middle Way Leadership   59

Chapter 8: Control   **63**

    A Title Does Not a Leader Make   63

    A Style to Suit You   69

    Stupid Things Business Owners Do   71

    Going from Bad Boss to Badass Boss   73

    Exercise: Leadership Mastery   75

    Exercise: Eight Questions   78

Chapter 9: Courage   **83**

    FAIL: First Attempt in Learning   84

    Exercise: The Mirror   88

Chapter 10: Creativity   **91**

    Hope is Not a Good Plan   93

    Organizational Identity   96

    Dashboards and Data   99

PART THREE: PUT PEOPLE FIRST   **103**

Chapter 11: Culture   **105**

    The Ship Makes the Pirate   106

    Create a Strengths-Based Culture   107

    The Right Stuff with Special Sauce   109

    Creating Loyal Fans   112

Chapter 12: Collaboration   **119**

    No Grit, No Pearl   120

    Bringing Out the Best in Others   124

    Increasing Employee Engagement   125

Chapter 13: Conflict   **129**

    Managing Stress   129

    Managing Emotions   132

    Managing Chaos   137

    Healthy Conflict   140

    Exercise: Peak Performance Primer   142

    Exercise: Healthy Conflict   144

PART FOUR: HOW TO BE EFFECTIVELY EFFICIENT   **149**

Chapter 14: Communication   **151**

The Power of Words   152

Sorry, I Had You on Mute   154

Meetings: Make Mine an Email, Please   156

My Circus, but Not My Monkeys   157

The Manual Makeover   162

Exercise: Wrong Way versus Right Way   164

Chapter 15: Competition   **167**

Blazing New Goat Trails   169

Always Be Evolving   172

Purpose Over Paycheck   176

Chapter 16: Choices   **179**

Belief Systems Are BS   179

Hoops and Hurdles   181

Change is a Choice   182

Manage the Why, Not Time   189

Competing Commitments   192

Getting Unstuck With a Mindset for Success   195

Jumping to Conclusions   198

Exercise: Stop Playing Whack-a-Mole   200

Exercise: Do the 180   204

Final Note   **206**

Appendix A: Build Your P&L from Scratch   *208*

Appendix B: The Best Marketing Bang for Your Buck   *210*

Appendix C: Glossary   *213*

Appendix D: Calculations   *214*

Appendix E: Key Performance Indicators (KPIs)   *216*

Acknowledgments   *220*

Recommended Reading   *224*

About the Author   *226*

Index   *228*

INTRODUCTION

If you own your business, you already know you're responsible for everything. Whether it's sales, financials, or operations, a person who owns 100 percent of a company wears all the hats. But in order to take your company to the next level, you need to do more, which is why you picked up this book. You need to develop innovative strategies to drive revenue growth. You need to learn skills, such as delegation, developing people, building high-functioning teams, creating a strengths-based culture, and streamlining processes. Along with managing others and working towards operational efficiency comes more responsibility and pressure. Many business owners struggle to find the time to manage everything and still maintain some semblance of work-life balance. Sound familiar?

My goal is to help you avoid the most common pitfalls that lead to failure. This book contains over thirty years of practical experience, along with evidence-based research, to help you elevate your business and surpass the competition. I know how because I've been there—I've been at the bottom, starting and failing multiple businesses, including reno-and-flip real estate, a vegan bakery, and a gaming software development company. And I've been at the top, having built a civil engineering company with thousands of dollars of debt to one with fifty employees and a multimillion-dollar annual revenue; ultimately, we landed a successful exit and were acquired by a venture capital firm.

Since then, I've followed my passion for helping other entrepreneurs grow and scale their businesses without all the blood, sweat, and tears I experienced along the way. If I can help prevent someone else from making the same mistakes I did, I figure it is time well spent.

Mess To Success

After going through the humiliation of being fired from a law firm, where I had been working as an administrative assistant, I was determined to find another job. I spent days driving from interview to interview in my beat-up Datsun without air-conditioning, roasting in the midday Miami sun.

Drenched in sweat and losing hope, I drove to the gas station, filled my tank, and went inside. I grabbed a bottle of vodka off the shelf, plopped it on the counter, and handed my credit card to the clerk. The clerk ran the charge through the machine, paused, and said he had to make a call. I wasn't paying attention until I saw him reach into a drawer, pull out a pair of scissors, and cut my card in half. I stood there, mouth open but unable to speak, as he handed me back the pieces of my lifeline. That plastic card was funding my whole existence. Then the adrenaline hit me.

"WHY DID YOU DO THAT?" I screamed.

"I just did what the credit card company told me to do. They told me to cut up your card," he said.

"BUT WHY?" I screamed again. "YOU DON'T UNDERSTAND. I need that card to live on!"

"I can't help you, lady. I don't know what to tell you. Why don't you ask them yourself?" He handed me the phone. "And you still need to pay for the gas."

I reached into my purse and tossed my change on the counter. I slammed the vodka down beside it.

"May I help the next person in line?" he said, glaring at me.

I drove home. I had enough money for food and gas to make it a couple of weeks, but without any job prospects, it didn't look good beyond that.

The following day, I was awakened by a phone call from a collection agency trying to force me to make a payment on my college loan. For weeks, they had been trying to track me down, all day, every day, like a juvenile delinquent making prank calls. I had charged over twenty thousand dollars worth of classes and still hadn't made a single payment. At the end of my first semester, I had ended up in the hospital for emergency surgery, and without health insurance, I was also facing thousands of dollars in medical bills.

I started selling my furniture and belongings for quick cash. I would have sold my blood if I wasn't so afraid of needles. I had just enough gas money to drive to job interviews and saved a little more by stealing toilet paper from gas station restrooms.

Then, instead of going to job interviews, I bought more vodka. I partied, stayed out late with my unemployed friends, and found other sketchy people to hang out with during the day. I suppose it boosted my ego to be around people worse off than me. But after a couple of weeks of numbing myself and avoiding reality, I had no more furniture to sell. I decided to swallow my pride and call my parents for help.

My parents owned a construction company and worked on projects at Whiteman Air Force Base, near Kansas City, Missouri. I had worked in the family business every summer, starting in second grade. Being the youngest, I had it easy compared to my older siblings. My mom taught me basic bookkeeping, and I learned about leadership and management from my dad. They were true entrepreneurs chasing the American dream. Both worked hard their whole life, and the company was the planet our family revolved around.

Asking them for help made me feel like a failure. I had left home at seventeen because I didn't want to live their life anymore. But they agreed to hire me for the summer so I could get back on my feet and start repaying my massive debts.

"It's just for the summer," I reiterated. I fully intended to return to Miami in the fall to finish my MBA and continue life on my terms.

My dad picked me up every morning while it was still oppressively dark, and we would drive in painful silence for an hour to the job site. One morning, he reached into the backseat and pulled a cassette out of a briefcase. I pretended to sleep and chuckled at how stupid it was that he had a briefcase full of motivational tapes. I never saw him as the kind of person who would take advice from anybody. No way, no how.

One morning, my dad popped in Brian Tracy's The Psychology of Achievement Classic,[1] and I heard something that made me sit up straight: "A sign of wisdom and maturity is when you come to terms with the realization that your decisions cause your rewards and consequences. You are responsible for your life, and your ultimate success depends on the choices you make."

---

1 Brian Tracy The *Psychology of Achievement Classic*, Nightingale-Conant, 1984. https://www.nightingale.com/psychology-achievement.html.

In an instant, I felt a shift in my reality. I saw that I had autonomy over my choices, and I could no longer blame the world out there for screwing things up.

My dad must have noticed. He turned down the sound and asked me what turned out to be a path-altering question.

"So what do you want to do with your life?" he asked.

"I don't know. That's a tough question."

"Why are you going to college?" he probed.

"I want to get an MBA and learn about business." I was worried about what he thought. I was the first in my family to get a bachelor's degree. Dad had a high school education and didn't see the value of college. He valued honest work for honest pay.

"What kind of business?"

"Any kind of business. I love business. I just want to own a business."

"Do you need an MBA to run a business?"

"Well, no. I guess not. A lot of the classes I was taking were based on theory. You know, what works theoretically."

"So, what's keeping you from doing that?

"What do you mean?"

"I mean, why don't you start your own business?"

"That's funny." I looked at him, but he wasn't laughing. "Well, I am learning how to do that in my classes."

"So if you want to own your own business, why don't you...just start a business? Learn by doing, not just by learning theories."

"Oh, okay. Sure. And how do you suggest I do that?"

"All you have to do is fill out incorporation papers, send them to the state, and you're in business."

"Where would I get the money?"

"I've got an idea. There's a service I need. If you're willing, I'm sure we can work out a deal to get you started."

"I can't wait to get a business card with my name on it and the title CEO in bold letters." I sat up even straighter, smiling.

"You should change your name from Pam to PJ. You'll have better luck getting your foot in the door in this male-dominated industry if they don't know you are a woman."

The Entrepreneur's Life

When people start companies, they envision a life of freedom—being their own boss, in charge of their schedule, working when they want to work. I wanted to create something I had complete control over, learn something new, and then move on to something better. I never envisioned owning a civil engineering company. But an accident that had happened years earlier was the catalyst.

In 1981, the Kansas City Hyatt Regency walkway collapse was one of the deadliest construction-related mishaps in U.S. history, killing 114 people and injuring 216. This led to several hearings and debates about the professional responsibilities of the engineers, fabricators, and contractors. Ultimately, the structural engineers were found guilty of gross negligence. The collapse resulted in a nationwide reexamination of building codes, and the American Society of Civil Engineering (ASCE) adopted a report giving structural engineers full responsibility for design projects.

There was a shift from contractors inspecting their own work to requiring an independent agency or inspector to oversee the project to ensure compliance with job site specifications. Initially, my company provided material testing services for new construction at Whiteman Air Force Base. Whiteman was home to the B-2 Stealth Bomber, later known as the Northrop Grumman B-2 Spirit, designed to avoid detection and interception during missions. The locals were excited about the hundreds of new jobs coming to the area, and they were talking about how the plane, with its cloaking technology, could literally vanish.

During my first month in business, I pounded the pavement and landed fourteen clients. I had naively agreed to eighteen-month contracts, so I wouldn't be returning to school in the fall. I didn't care. I was exploring the world of entrepreneurship and living the dream.

My first year in business was a success. I enjoyed a windfall of cash, which I stockpiled under my mattress. My mom came over one day, and I said, "Mom, guess what I'm doing?" I spread all the cash on the bed and rolled on it. "I'm rolling in cash. Get it?"

She thought it was hilarious, too, and ran to get my dad so he could see for himself.

I thought things would only get easier and easier. As they say, ignorance is bliss. It was around year two when I learned the truth: owning a business takes hard work and determination. Just when you think you have everything figured out, a calamity awaits.

The first employee I hired hurt his back bending over to pick up an empty bucket. I was watching from the window inside the trailer when it happened. In that moment, it looked almost comical. But worker's comp didn't think it was funny. My insurance rates went through the roof. I needed to replace him, but the state Division of Labor called to tell me I couldn't fire him and I had to find him another job. Since he couldn't lift anything or go out to job sites, the only position left was mine. He came in every morning, put his feet on the desk, read the paper, drank coffee, smoked cigarettes, and clocked out at 5:00 on the dot every evening.

Meanwhile, I had to do his work, which included hauling materials at job sites. One morning, it was below freezing and snowing sideways. Whatever I was carrying was heavy, and I slipped and fell right on my face in the mud. I just lay there crying. Reality had crept up on me. I not only had a company but a job, and the job had taken over like a kudzu vine, devouring the fun from my life. I was working eighty hours a week just to keep up. The mattress cash was put to work feeding the company to keep it alive and paying my employee to catch up on the news.

At some point, most entrepreneurs struggle with two things: dwindling cash and never having enough time. You wonder why you keep spending time making improvements to move the needle, but nothing changes. Finding the happy place between profit and loss is like waiting for pigs to fly. You get stuck in the day-to-day minutiae, and nothing seems to increase your bottom line. You dream of having better clients, quality staff, and time for yourself. How could that be so hard?

This is the stage when many entrepreneurs get into the habit of doing everything themselves. They believe they will save time and money that way because they don't trust anyone else to do the job as well as they can. They get trapped in a loop of fixing whatever comes up that day, that moment—shooting from the hip, bang, bang. Whether it's spending time on problems that need to be dealt with quickly or chasing down a new customer, it's a vicious cycle that's hard to break. What ends up happening, though, is the company stops growing. When you're that close to the action, you don't realize you are sabotaging your own potential to be productive.

Three years in, I decided to get a bank loan—because money solves everything, right? After weeks of preparing my documents and pitching them to the banker, though, my twelve-thousand-dollar request was denied. The banker politely told me I should probably consider a different career. Crushed but motivated, I left determined to prove him wrong.

In year four, a major competitor contacted me for a meeting. I invited him to the office space I was renting in a garage behind an auto parts store in a town with a population of barely two thousand.

"Why do you want to buy me out? What's in it for me?" I asked. I was genuinely curious since I was struggling to make a profit and basically a day away from looking for that new career the banker had suggested.

"Think about it. If I buy you out, you could work for me. I could teach you in one year what it took me twenty years to learn."

I watched him drive away in his luxury sedan and thought about how lovely working out of a real office would be. I ultimately declined the offer, along with my dream of being rescued and retiring my boots for high heels. But what he said about learning stuck with me.

I went on to grow my company, and eventually we were making millions in annual revenue. After two decades, I sold it to a venture capitalist on a handshake. And over the years, I learned a few frameworks and principles that have never failed me. If you learn and follow them, too, you'll be well on your way to launching the business of your dreams or leveling up your current leadership skills and path to success.

There are 32.5 million small businesses with fewer than 250 employees in the United States, or 99.9 percent of all businesses. Only 9 percent of those small businesses make over 1 million dollars annually, 16 percent of their owners make only $10,000 per year, and 50 percent of small businesses fail in the first five years. It could be because of a lack of demand, not having the right team in place, a poor business model, ignoring customers, and ineffective marketing. But the biggest reason, the reason that 82 percent of small US businesses fail is cash flow—not enough cash to pay bills, support their owners, and invest back into the company.[2]

The pandemic caused a dramatic shift in traditional employment, although the writing was on the wall for a while. Major shifts create opportunities; they make the world is ripe for change. Adopting new strategies and leadership initiatives that honor better life-work integration or lifestyle is what I call the Middle Way toward best practices for best outcomes.

In the first part of this book, we are going to focus on day-to-day, bottom-line concerns that are central to getting your business on the right track and keeping it there. We will discuss how to grow and scale your business by mastering the profit and loss report, among other brass tacks. Maybe your eyes are already glazing over, but trust me when I say that getting clear on the financials is the single most important thing you can do to elevate your company and keep it in the black. I'll break it down in a way that is accessible and immediately executable. This way, you can start making improvements to the way you run your business today.

In the final sections, we are going to dive deep into leadership and the ways to optimize your people and processes. The idea of leadership can feel abstract, but it is no less critical than your fiscal awareness, and you'll soon see that there are many possible approaches you can take to galvanize your team to reach for greatness.

---

2 Luisa Zhou, *Small Business Statistics: The Ultimate List in 2023*, https://www.luisazhou.com/blog/small-business-statistics/.

No matter what stage of business development you're at, whether you are a startup or a mature company, you will find practical resources to level up both your financial and leadership skills to become a mission-driven CEO.

As you go through the book, I highly recommend you have a notebook, pen, and paper, or a notes app handy to take advantage of the exercises, journaling, and reflection opportunities throughout. Any time you're unsure of the terminology I'm using, flip to Appendix B, which defines the expert lingo you'll need to learn.

Let's start with one of the best exercises a business owner can do—an annual business assessment. When you take a step back from the day-to-day minutiae and really focus on your long-term big-picture goals, you can easily identify ways to grow by creating actionable steps to improve your business. The assessment will also help you get an accurate picture of ways to enhance your organization's strengths and minimize its weaknesses.

BUSINESS ASSESSMENT FORM

Name of company: _____

Years in business:_____

State your elevator pitch (a few sentences about the company that spark interest):

_____

_____

_____

_____

_____

_____

What are the top three strengths of your company?

1. _____

2. _____

3. _____

What are the top three weaknesses of your company?

1. _____

2. _____

3. _____

What are the opportunities for your company?

1. _____

2. _____

3. _____

What are the threats to your company?

_____

_____

_____

_____

_____

_____

_____

_____

What are the problems you are facing (Check all that apply):

☐ Poor leadership or management decisions

☐ Autocratic or overextended management

☐ Ineffective or nonexistent communications

☐ Inefficient compensation and incentive programs

☐ Company goals are not understood or executed.

☐ Business is stagnant or deteriorating.

☐ Business is in the growth stage but growth is uncontrollable.

☐ Insufficient marketing analysis or research

☐ Poor sales approach or processes

☐ Poor customer service or customer needs are ignored.

☐ Financial reporting is not accurate or timely.

☐ Lack of capital or premature scaling

☐ History of failed expansion plans, lack of planning

☐ Excessive regulations, inability to stay compliant, high taxation, or high-interest rates

☐ Inability to compete with similar businesses, nodifferentiation

Check which reports you currently have in place and which are up-to-date. Circle the reports you need to develop:

- ☐ Budget versus actual
- ☐ Cash flow statement
- ☐ Income and balance sheet (Profit and Loss)
- ☐ Accounts receivable aging report
- ☐ Revenue projects
- ☐ Net profit margin over time
  - ☐ Sales analysis
  - ☐ Sales/growth projection

Check which of the following you need to develop and number by priority:

- ☐ Marketing strategy and analysis
- ☐ Sales processes
- ☐ Customer experience playbook
- ☐ Quality control procedures
- ☐ HR, employee benefits, policies, onboarding
- ☐ New product/services launch plan
- ☐ Health and safety/OSHA compliance

- ☐ Other, explain: _____

_____

_____

_____

_____

_____

_____

Do you have any of the following financial key performance indicators (KPIs)[3] in place? Circle any you'd like to develop:

- ☐ MRR (monthly recurring revenue)
- ☐ Net profit margin
- ☐ Gross profit margin
- ☐ Cash flow
- ☐ Current accounts receivable and accounts payable process
- ☐ Inventory turnover

Marketing

Please describe your target market.

_____

_____

_____

_____

_____

_____

_____

_____

_____

_____

_____

---

3 Laura Hennigan, What is A KPI? Definition & Examples, Forbes Advisor, Apr 24, 2023. https://www.forbes.com/advisor/business/what-is-a-kpi-definition-examples/.

Describe your ideal customer.

_____

_____

_____

_____

_____

_____

Do you have a written marketing plan that you adhere to?

_____

_____

What are you using to sell your products or services?

_____

_____

_____

_____

_____

_____

_____

_____

What percentage of your customers make repeat purchases from you?

_____

What type of systematic follow-up system (if any) do you use to contact potential customers at regular intervals to mature and convert them into paying clients?

_____

_____

_____

_____

_____

_____

_____

Check if you have any of the following marketing KPIs in place, or circle if you are interested in developing or improving this factor:

- ☐ Marketing campaign effectiveness
- ☐ Direct traffic
- ☐ Pages per visit
- ☐ Unsubscribe rate
- ☐ Cart abandon rate

Customer Experience (CX)

Please check any of the following issues you are experiencing.

- ☐ Unable to provide value/usability/relevance of the product for the customer
- ☐ Inadequate/insufficient user-onboarding support
- ☐ Inadequate user enablement (or training)
- ☐ Poor customer experience or support
- ☐ Budgetary problems
- ☐ Competition releasing disruptive/new features

Check any of the following CX KPIs you have in place.
Circle those you'd like to develop.

- ☐ Customer acquisition rate
- ☐ First call resolution (FCR)
- ☐ Customer wait time
- ☐ Monthly recurring revenue (MRR), by customer
- ☐ Customer churn rate
- ☐ Net promoter score (NPS)
- ☐ Customer satisfaction score (CSAT)
- ☐ Client retention rate
- ☐ Employee engagement

Sales

Do you have a referral program in place? _____

What joint ventures, partnerships, or strategic alliances does your company have in place?

_____

_____

_____

_____

_____

_____

_____

_____

_____

Describe your current sales process. How does a lead typically become a prospect and then become a customer?

_____

_____

_____

_____

_____

_____

_____

_____

Do you have a clearly defined, written sales plan that generates leads and closes sales? _____

How often do you follow up with prospects?

☐ Every day
☐ Once a week
☐ Once a month
☐ Once a quarter
☐ Once a year

What do you do with the prospects you don't close?

_____

_____

_____

What kind of sales training is currently available?

_____

_____

_____

_____

_____

_____

Check any of the following Sales KPIs you have in place. If not, circle which ones you are interested in developing.

- ☐ New business per period
- ☐ LTV (lifetime value of customer)
- ☐ Number of engaged qualified leads in sales funnel
- ☐ Hours of resources spent on sales follow-up
- ☐ Average time for conversion
- ☐ Net sales/dollar amount or percentage growth
- ☐ Sales closing ratio

What are the most frequently stated objections when selling to large clients?

_____

_____

_____

_____

_____

_____

_____

What is your step-by-step process for follow-up with a client after they buy?

_____

_____

_____

_____

_____

_____

_____

_____

_____

_____

_____

What do you perceive as the top three challenges right now?

1. _____
2. _____
3. _____

Your top three competitors:

1. _____
2. _____
3. _____

Describe WHY you are in business.

_____

_____

_____

_____

_____

_____

_____

Is there anything else you'd like to add about your business that would help evaluate your circumstances?

_____

_____

_____

_____

_____

_____

Keep this assessment handy as you read, and return to it often—especially a few months down the line after reading this book and implementing any changes in your business that feel aligned with your vision and mission.

PART ONE

How to Make Financials Your Superpower

Chapter 1

CASH

"Chase the vision, not the money;
the money will end up following you."
—Tony Hsieh, Zappos CEO[4]

D id you know that some of the most common phobias are karaoke, public speaking, and doing math? Well, I'm not sure whether it's true about math, but at one time it was true for me.

When I started my business, I was advised to hire an accountant. He was patient and taught me how to read what the numbers on the spreadsheet were telling me. I was lucky to have him because he taught me in a way that helped me gain an appreciation for financials and learn how numbers could forecast the future. This allowed me to control and anticipate revenues and expenses and grow my business in a strategic way. Ultimately, financials became my superpower.

Understanding business math and financial principles is key to being a great business owner. In this section, we're going to learn to do a quick and simple analysis of your finances and expenses so you can be more confident about running your business. You will also learn tips and tricks to understand your financials in a way that will increase cash flow and profitability.

---

4 https://en.wikipedia.org/wiki/Tony_Hsieh.

Interpreting the numbers in your profit and loss statement (P&L) can be overwhelming. But this section will teach you to love math as much as I do. Don't worry if you don't have any bookkeeping procedures or financials in place. We'll go over how to develop these.

- Over the next few chapters, you will learn how to:

- Simplify and uncomplicate the profit and loss statement.

- Get a quick pulse on your business.

- Explore ways to increase your revenue.

- Discover quick ways to lower your cost of goods sold

- Examine techniques to lower your overhead.

- Use the information you gather to increase profitability.

- Forecast future economic trends.

- Use tools to help you make easier decisions.

- Create growth opportunities for your business.

Profit and Loss

Before we dive in, let's agree on the key terms and calculations of the profit and loss statement, also known as the P&L, which can vary according to personal preference.

Let's begin by defining key P&L terms:

Revenue, also known as gross income, refers to your sales. Top-line growth happens when you increase your sales over a period of time.

Cost of goods sold (COGS) is called "variable costs" because they are prone to fluctuate over a period of time.

Gross profit is calculated by subtracting COGS from revenue. This figure is essential because it represents the funds that you will use to pay for overhead.

Gross profit percentage is calculated by dividing gross profit by revenue, multiplied by 100.

Overhead, also called "fixed costs," are the bills you must pay every month, whether you make a sale or not. These are the bills you pay that are fixed and always roughly the same amount. They're what I call "keep the doors open and the lights on" expenses, such as rent, utilities, and insurance.

Net profit is derived from gross profit minus overhead; it's also known as net income or the bottom line. You can think of it as total income minus all expenses. Bottom-line growth is an indicator of how efficient a business is at controlling costs.

Net profit percentage is calculated by dividing net profit by revenue, multiplied by 100.

Definitions and Calculations
Revenue: Also known as "gross" revenue, refers to what's sold and income derived from it.
COGS: Cost of goods sold. The variable material and labor costs incurred when selling a product or service
Gross profit: Revenue – COGs
Gross profit %: Gross profit ÷ revenue × 100
Overhead: Fixed bills to be paid, whether there are sales or not
Net profit: Gross profit – overhead
Net profit %: Net profit ÷ revenue × 100

Table 1.1: The essential language of your financials.

Of course, there are many more calculations and ratios you can use to monitor your business, and additional terms that accountants and CPAs use, but we are going to focus on the basics. Be sure to check out the Appendices for a glossary and valuable calculations that will help you become acquainted with terms we will use throughout the book.

Next, let's dive into the numbers and terms of a P&L. To help you understand them, we'll use a hypothetical pet supply company called DogToyz, and we'll make up the numbers of this company's P&L. Let's say that the company has been in business for eighteen months and one of the dog toys has recently gone viral. Now the CEO, Jenn, is scrambling to make sure they can fill the orders. She knows it's hard to prepare for a moment of internet fame, but she's been dreaming of this opportunity and created a strategy to capitalize on the momentum she's built. Anticipating that things will move fast, she focuses on getting a handle on the cash flow and profit so she can fund the growth that will be required.

Here's a snapshot of the DogToyz year-end P&L:

Description	Amount
Revenue	$400,000
Cost of goods sold	$220,000
Gross profit	$180,000
Gross profit %	45%
Overhead	$80,000
Net profit	$100,000
Net profit %	25%

Table 1.2: DogToyz annual profit and loss statement.

To make financials your superpower, we are going to simplify things. And when it comes to interpreting the numbers and using them to grow your business, there are only three you need to focus on:

revenue, COGS, and overhead. That's because these numbers are the ones that can make or break your company. The four other numbers (gross profit, gross profit %, net profit, net profit %) are derived from the other three.

Revenue

Last year, DogToyz made $400,000. That represents the gross income brought in from all the sales over twelve months. This number is promising and shows that the business has the ability to sell products, something investors are interested in. Let's check it out.

Revenue Evaluation

Let's say Jenn, the CEO of DogToyz and her partner, Susan, went on Shark Tank. They decided to ask for $200,000 in exchange for 10 percent ownership. And they decided to value the company at $2,000,000 since one-tenth of the company equals $200,000, and ten-tenths (or 100 percent) equals $2 million.

The Sharks ask for the previous year sales. Since DogToyz is currently bringing in $400,000 a year, they calculate that it would take five years to reach $2 million.

But the Sharks are also curious if Jenn has any future sales that might make the company more appealing. She's happy to tell them that they recently landed a deal with Chewy, which has agreed to purchase $500,000 worth of products in the next year. This would be even more attractive to the investors since there are sales in the pipeline, an almost guaranteed win-win.

Yes, it looks like a great investment, but the Sharks want to know more. Just because a company has revenue doesn't mean it is generating a profit. In fact, many businesses are good at making millions but at the end of the year show a loss on their P&L. If DogToyz were making $400,000 in sales but spending $395,000, this would be a red flag.

Earnings Multiple

The Sharks want to know what the profit is to calculate an earnings multiple. For example, if the company is valued at $2 million and has a profit of $200,000, the company would have an earnings multiple of 10, or $2 million ÷ $200,000. Is that good or bad? We don't know without comparing it to other companies in the same sector or industry. Let's say the dog toy industry has an average earnings multiple of 12. At 12x earnings, this would value the business at $2.4 million, or 12 × $200,000. It's fair to say that this valuation is good for the Sharks. There are many other ways to value a business, and I'd recommend that you investigate those on your own.

It's been said that it's a good idea to build a business with selling in mind. I wish someone had given me this advice. Why? Because when it came time for me to sell my company, it took me two years. Be forewarned: From creating the acquisition plan to the actual sale, the whole process can take up to five years or longer.

Cost Of Goods Sold

The next important number is cost of goods sold (COGS). COGS represents the total of all the costs used to create and sell a product or deliver a service. These costs include labor (direct and contractual), materials, packaging, shipping, and sales commissions. In most cases, COGS will increase as your sales volume increases.

If you are a professional service provider, such as a financial planner, lawyer, consultant, accountant, or chiropractor, you won't typically incur any costs in what you are selling, so you won't have COGS. We will focus on ways to impact revenue and overhead since COGS won't be in play.

As a side note, the average gross profit margin for professional service organizations can range from 25 percent to 40 percent. An individual consultant can make between a 50 percent and 100 percent gross profit margin. That means that for every dollar made, 100 percent of it is straight profit.

Overhead

Overhead is also called fixed costs. Overhead covers everything you have to pay, whether you made a sale or not. It is what it takes to turn the lights on and all the rest of the daily, weekly, and monthly expenses required to operate. These costs are considered "fixed" because they stay the same and recur each month. These include such recurring expenses as rent, insurance, utilities, office supplies, office salaries, general maintenance, advertising, janitorial services, and anything related to your automobiles.

Now let's look at ways you can impact revenue, COGS, and overhead by making small, incremental changes to get big results.

Increasing Revenue

Let's set some goals, get strategic, and see what happens when we make changes to revenue, COGS, and overhead. We will do this by either increasing or decreasing the numbers and seeing what kind of effect it has on our cash flow and net profit.

Let's set a quarterly goal of increasing our revenue by 5 percent. Our DogToyz company's original revenue was $400,000, so a 5 percent increase would increase that number to $420,000. Our COGS stays the same at $220,000, but our gross profit has risen from $180,000 to $200,000. This increases our gross profit share from 45 percent to 50 percent. Our bills are fixed, which means our overhead doesn't change, remaining the same at $80,000. But we see an increase in our net profit from $100,000 to $120,000. It's amazing how a small percentage increase in revenue gives us a $20,000 gain in our net profits.

Description	Change	Result
Revenue	$400,000	$420,000
Cost of goods sold	$220,000	$220,000
Gross profit	$180,000	$200,000
Gross profit %	45%	50%
Overhead	$80,000	$80,000
Net profit	$100,000	$120,000
Net profit %	25%	29%

Table 1.3: If we increase our revenue by 5%, our profit rises by $20,000

Reducing COGS

Let's do the same with our COGS to show how a 5 percent decrease can increase our bottom line. Our revenue is $400,000, but our COGS go from $220,000 to $209,000. This small change affects our gross profit, which goes from $180,000 to $191,000. And it gives us an increase in gross profit percentage of 2.75 percent (i.e., from 45 percent to 47.75 percent). The overhead remains $80,000, but the net profit increases from $100,000 to $111,000. We've just added $11,000 to our bottom line by decreasing our COGS just 5 percent.

Description	Change	Result
Revenue	400,000	400,000
Cost of goods sold	220,000	209,000
Gross profit	180,000	191,000
Gross profit %	45%	47.75%
Overhead	80,000	80,000
Net profit	100,000	111,000
Net profit %	25%	28%

Table 1.4: Reducing COGS by 5% results in an $11,000 increase in net profit

Reducing Overhead

What if we lower our overhead by 5 percent? The revenue, COGS, gross profit, and gross profit percentage remain the same. But if we cut overhead costs by 5 percent, we go from $80,000 to $76,000 in overhead, and our net profit increases from $100,000 to $104,000. This adds $4,000 to our bottom line.

Description	Change	Result
Revenue	400,000	400,000
Cost of goods sold	220,000	220,000
Gross profit	180,000	180,000
Gross profit %	45%	45%
Overhead	80,000	76,000
Net profit	100,000	104,000
Net profit %	25%	26%

Table 1.5: Lowering overhead by 5% increases our net profit by $4,000

You can see how making small tweaks gives us big results. So you can imagine how making larger adjustments would give you even bigger results.

The Magic Formula

Now look at what happens when we change all three. When we increase revenue and reduce COGS and overhead by 5 percent, revenue increases from $400,000 to $420,000, our COGS decreases from $220,000 to $209,000, and our overhead drops from $80,000 to $76,000.

Description	Change	Result
Revenue	400,000	420,000
Cost of goods sold	220,000	209,000
Gross profit	180,000	211,000
Gross profit %	45%	50%
Overhead	80,000	76,000
Net profit	100,000	135,000
Net profit %	25%	32%

Table 1.6: A 5% shift in revenue, COGS, and overhead increases net profit

Even small changes move the needle and put us in a more favorable financial position. Our bottom line has increased by $35,000. Our gross profit shot up from $180,000 to $211,000, and our gross profit percentage increased by 5 percent. In the end, we profited $35,000.

A lot of entrepreneurs panic when their sales drop or their expenses increase. The first thing they want to do is focus on marketing. They think they will solve their financial problems by spending money on a splashy campaign. Nothing against a good marketing strategy, but that is a long game. This exercise proves that making small shifts in revenue, COGS, and overhead will increase your bottom line without having to spend a dime. These increases are not a one-time bump like an advertisement. They can continue to generate profit in perpetuity.

Take time to look at your P&L and see where you might make some small changes to impact your bottom line. If you don't currently have a P&L, check out Appendix A to get started building one.

Finally, a brief note on collections and accounts receivable. This is something that business owners tend to overlook until they run into trouble. My recommendation would be to set up a collection policy early and stick to it. This means someone will be making collection calls on a monthly or weekly basis, whichever makes the most sense. Stay on top of accounts that are slow paying, and don't let them get near the danger zone, which kicks in when collections are more than ninety days past due.

Chapter 2
CAPITAL

"Having a vision for what you want is not enough. Vision without execution is hallucination." —Thomas A. Edison[5]

In the previous chapter, we proved that small incremental changes to your revenue will result in an increase in sales. In this chapter, we will look at different options for raising gross revenue, which means increasing top-line growth. But how exactly do we make this happen?

To increase sales, you need more sales. That may seem obvious, but I've worked with a lot of business owners who tell me how much they hate sales, even though they are solely responsible for making the sales. When they started their company, they did everything—they spent time building relationships, providing quality customer service, and being the main point of contact. As they grew, they wanted to delegate sales. What they so often failed to realize was that without the proper processes in place, they were setting themselves up for disaster. I've heard it so many times: "I just want to automate everything so I can remove myself from the day-to-day minutiae. I'm going to put X in charge of sales."

But X doesn't have any skin in the game, doesn't care about the customer, and hasn't been trained in sales. Weeks go by before the owner, who has been enjoying some time off, realizes there has been a

---

5 https://en.wikipedia.org/wiki/Thomas_Edison.

huge decline in monthly sales. This is not something that is a quick fix. It can take a while for the company to recover.

Top-Line Growth

Let's look at strategies besides making more sales to increase top-line growth. One of the easiest ways to increase revenue is to increase pricing. But is it the smartest option? I've seen business owners cringe at the idea of raising their prices and so they haven't done it in years. They get hung up on the idea they will lose most, if not all, of their customers.

To avoid that trap, I got into the habit of making small, incremental price increases at the beginning of every year. My engineering company was growing fast, but so was the cost of doing business. I wanted to pay my professional engineers and special inspectors a competitive wage and provide decent benefits so they could make a good living and take care of their families. But with rising insurance rates, inflation, and taxes, it was a challenge to balance cash flow, especially when we were experiencing high-growth phases.

By raising prices, did I lose customers? Probably. But they weren't the ideal customers. They were the ones that shopped around for the lowest price they could find. I didn't mind letting those headaches go straight to my competitors. I retained loyal customers who understood we would provide prompt, quality service but were also in business to make a profit. People will pay more for the reassurance that they don't have to worry about getting the value and service they expect.

Run the numbers and consider how many clients you can afford to lose with a small price increase and still break even. Consider the possibility that you could be making the same revenue as before but with fewer, better, premier customers.

Increase Prices or Cut Costs

Which option would benefit us the most: raising prices or cutting costs? Let's find out. How much of an increase in revenue by raising our prices would it take to achieve a $20,000 increase in profits?

On the DogToyz P&L, we have a 45 percent gross profit, which means that every dollar in sales results in $0.45 in profit. If we divide $20,000 by 0.45, we get $44,444. This means that to get a $20,000 increase in profits through a change in price, you would need to produce $44,444 in additional revenue. Instead, if we lower our overhead by 20 percent, from $80,000 to $64,000, we see an increase in our net profit of $16,000 without increasing revenue. I know you might be thinking this sounds like pie in the sky, but hear me out.

Raising prices: A luxury dog toy retailer might have a loyal and affluent customer base that values their high-quality, exclusive products. To increase revenue, this retailer could raise the prices of their most popular products. They could justify the price increase by highlighting the premium materials, superior craftsmanship, and added value that the products provide. If the retailer's demand is relatively inelastic, customers will continue to purchase their products despite the price increase. If the retailer can achieve a price increase that results in an additional $44,444 in revenue, they will see their desired $20,000 increase in profits.

Cutting costs: The same retailer might identify inefficiencies in their production or supply chain that they can address to lower overhead costs. For example, they could negotiate better rates with suppliers, streamline their manufacturing process to reduce waste, or optimize their logistics for lower shipping costs. Alternatively, they could reduce administrative costs by automating certain tasks or reducing energy consumption in their facilities. By implementing these measures, the retailer could achieve a 20% reduction in overhead from $80,000 to $64,000, resulting in a $16,000 increase in net profit without needing to increase revenue.

Of course, each of these strategies has its own potential risks and benefits. Raising prices could deter price-sensitive customers and potentially hurt sales volume, while cutting costs could potentially compromise product quality or employee morale if not handled carefully. The optimal approach will depend on the specific circumstances of the business, their market, and their customers.

Description	Change	Result
Revenue	$400,000	$400,000
Cost of goods sold	$220,000	$220,000
Gross profit	$180,000	$180,000
Gross profit %	45%	45%
Overhead	$80,000	$64,000
Net profit	$100,000	$116,000
Net profit %	25%	29%

Table 2.1: Lowering overhead increases net profit

Remember this: By whatever amount you reduce overhead costs, 100 percent of that dollar amount goes to your bottom line. This proves that reducing overhead has a greater impact on your bottom-line results than increasing revenue.

Sell More Stuff

Selling more seems like the obvious way to increase revenue. But how do you go about selling more stuff? Again, most people think that marketing will solve everything. They don't realize it takes a long time to implement a plan, which often makes this the least effective approach for immediate results.

Keep in mind that your target customers are inundated with marketing messages every day. I've heard that you have to reach customers with marketing touches at least seventeen times before they begin to pay attention—that is, if they don't block or unsubscribe from your emails at the first point of contact.

A better solution is to focus on building out a sales plan. Start by tracking how many times you contact prospects. Are you asking them if they're ready to buy, or are you providing value and letting your product or service sell itself? Most companies' sales strategy is to focus on the features and benefits of their products or services while forgetting to talk about how they plan to provide extraordinary value. Don't get hung up on giving your customer what you think they need. Ask your customer what's important to them and then provide a solution. You can learn a lot from unhappy customers, too.

Sales Playbook

A sales playbook is the handbook used to train your sales team. It captures the best processes and communicates your strategy to the team to ensure consistency in delivery. It lays out various scenarios so there is clarity regarding what to do in different situations.

A simple sales process begins with finding prospects, obtaining a list of leads, and putting them in a sales pipeline. A sales pipeline delineates the steps you will take to convert a contact to a customer.

When you get a prospective lead, you also want to make sure to prequalify them. You want to know they can afford what you are selling and are the right fit for what you are offering. If you skip this step, you may waste a lot of time or money, only to find out they are not your ideal customer and don't want what you're selling.

Before you create a sales plan or playbook, define your target audience and determine where to find them. Take time to map out the qualities of a buyer persona that detail not only demographics but psychographics, which are behind the reasons why people buy what they buy.

When you've identified your ideal customer, based on the ones that you love to work with, aim to attract more of the same. Focus on a small community and then empower them to help you reach bigger and better markets. Find the congregation points and the common interest areas, such as where they go to share and learn from people in their industry. Research what meetings, conferences, podcasts, social media, influencers, magazines, and newsletters they follow or subscribe to.

Whether you are giving demos, providing trial discounts, or engaging prospects with creatively crafted scripts, make sure to track your progress so you can adapt. Consider interviewing your current clients to discover what they value most about your company. This is how you develop a good reputation for word-of-mouth advertising.

A sales funnel, meanwhile, is the journey you take prospective customers through. It starts the minute you get their attention and they become aware that you exist.

Once you attract their interest in your product or service, you want to move them to the next stage, which is evaluating whether you are a good fit and can satisfy their needs. Next comes the negotiation stage of price and terms, and then you close the sale by getting payment. But don't stop there—stay top of mind and renew their interest so they will repurchase.

Having a good customer relationship management tool (CRM) will help you stay organized and efficient and will allow you to track your success rate. A CRM can be as simple as an Excel spreadsheet, or it can be expensive software tailored to your industry.

Here are the steps to creating a sales plan:

- Set your goals and objectives.
- Create a sales budget.
- Create key performance indicators (KPIs) to track progress (see the Appendix for a list of KPIs).
- Implement sales tools.
- Implement CRM systems.
- Institute proposal-generation systems.
- Develop a sales pipeline to identify leads and prospects.
- Create a sales funnel through which you will take leads during your sales process.
- Set up demos.
- Create sales scripts to use in different scenarios, including emails, in-person meetings, initial calls, follow-up calls, and so on.
- Launch an email drip campaign.
- Track conversion rates that quantify the path from lead to conversion and close.
- Test, track, and tweak performance and results.
- Create a client retention strategy.

Pump Up the Volume

If you want to sell more, you need to increase the volume of buyers. To get new customers, forming partnerships or relationships, such as affiliates or joint ventures should be at the top of your list.

Find partners who serve similar clients that need or want what you sell to create a win-win environment for both parties. Affiliates can be individuals, organizations, or businesses. Joint ventures involve two or more businesses that form a partnership to share their market or endorse a specific product or service to their customer base. Usually, a revenue share arrangement is made in such cases.

Here are some steps to setting up partnerships:

- Make a list of every product or service that people might use before, during, and after they use yours.

- Locate businesses that provide these products or services, and talk to them about how you could support each other's ventures.

- Create a well-crafted email, pick up the phone, or make a personal visit to find the ideal businesses that are excited about partnering with you.

A successful chiropractor I know told me a story of how she was able to grow her business by partnering with an acupuncturist. She told me, "I knew I needed to bring in more volume." If more people were coming through the door, she found she had a better chance of converting them to use her services. And it worked. Michelle Robin is now one of the most successful chiropractors in Kansas City.

Upsell, Cross-Sell, and Down-Sell

Upselling is a sales technique used to encourage customers to spend more by purchasing the higher grade, larger quantity, or bigger size of an item they intended to buy anyway. The classic example is when you order at McDonald's and they ask, "Want to supersize that meal?"

Cross-selling is the process of getting customers to purchase products or services in addition to the original items they intended to purchase. These products are often complementary, so they are more likely to appeal to the customer, as in, "Do you want fries with that?"

Down-selling is a strategy to offer alternatives to customers that can't afford what you are selling. It's a way to get them over the finish line. Once they become your customer, you work to provide as much value as possible. By doing that, you're proving that you are motivated to find ways to best serve them. What's more, someone who bought a product from you is likely to continue to buy from you and become a long-term loyal customer. There's a good chance they will be a good referrals source, too. Once you've shown your value and created a fan, you can always upsell or cross-sell at a future date.

If your customer rejects your first upsell attempt, offer a different, lower-priced item, or offer the same item at a slightly lower price with add-ons or bonuses. To be effective, a down-sell needs to be low enough that customers don't think twice about whether they should make the purchase because it's such a good deal.

Accounts Receivable

Accounts receivable (AR) is the amount owed to a company resulting from the company providing goods and/or services on credit. Businesses often lose track of accounts receivable by giving their customers too long a time frame to pay for work that has been completed. If you allow your customers to pay on a 30- or 45-day time frame, this can easily start slipping into a 60- and 90-day period. When this happens, your cash flow is negatively impacted. You are basically acting as a bank for your customer.

One thing that used to drive me crazy was the amount of money in our accounts receivable that was past due. We did a lot of work for state and city municipalities, which are notoriously slow at paying. Their accounts would hover in the 120-day past-due range. My bank was willing to give me a line of credit but told me that they would only base it on current AR and that anything past 90 days is considered uncollectible.

Here are some tips to help you get your accounts receivable under control:

- Itemize and review your AR so you know who owes what and when.

- Prioritize which clients are a risk, based on past payment history.

- Set up a time to call all past-due accounts weekly; a simple reminder is often all it takes.

- Set up a tracking and notification system.

- Reconsider if "30 days net" payments make sense, or if giving a discount for early payment makes sense.

- Consider hiring a collection agency. They take a big percentage but do all the heavy lifting for you.

- Sadly, people will take advantage of you if you let them. When you provide a product or a service, you deserve to be paid on time. It is more than reasonable to request payment upon delivery and give a two-week window so that you receive prompt compensation. You've worked hard, so don't lose track of your money.

Now that we've highlighted the options for improving top-line growth—including cutting costs, selling more, forming partnerships, and increasing prices—we're going to look at the cost of goods sold and provide practical applications to drive performance and create even more impact.

Chapter 3

COGS

"If you pay peanuts, you get monkeys." —*Sir James Goldsmith*[6]

In this chapter, we will talk about the cost of goods sold and the things that impact them. As we discussed in Chapter 1, both revenue and COGS directly impact gross profit. Your gross profit pays your overhead and generates net profit in your business. So, let's talk about the many ways we can lower COGS and increase profits in the process.

Pricing

One of the hardest decisions business owners face is pricing products and services correctly. When developing a pricing strategy, we need to understand gross margin and profit. A lot of business owners make the mistake of guesstimating what their profit should be.

Let's look back to our pet supply company. Say our costs to make a dog bed, including the cost of materials and labor, is $50. We randomly decide we want to generate a 35 percent profit. If you multiply the cost to make the dog bed by 1.35, you get 50.00 × 1.35, or $67.50. So we will make a 35 percent profit if we raise our price to $67.50 per dog bed. But does this price strategy make sense? Let's find out.

---

6 https://www.sirja mesgoldsmith.com/

If we subtract our COGS from our revenue, we get a gross profit of $17.50 (67.50 − 50.00 = 17.50). And, if we divide $17.50 by 67.50 (17.50 ÷ 67.50 × 100 = 25.9 percent), our gross profit percentage is only 26 percent. This means we are only generating about 75 percent of the profit we were aiming for, which, in turn, means multiplying our COGS by 1.35 (35 percent) is the wrong approach.

To find the correct number, we use the inverse of 35 percent, which is 65 percent. You get the inverse by taking the profit margin we want and subtracting it from one (1 - 0.35 = 0.65).

So now, if we take our COGS of $50 and divide it by 0.65, we get $76.92. By pricing our new dog bed at $76.92, we reach a profit margin of 35%. Our price is $76.93. We subtract our COGS of $50 from our revenue, and we get a gross profit of $26.92 for each dog bed sold. If we divide 26.92 (profit) by $76.92 (revenue), we get 35 percent.

This is the right way to calculate the desired profit margin:

$76.92 (revenue) − 50 (COGS) = 26.92 (profit)

$26.92 (profit) ÷ 76.92 (revenue) × 100 = 35%

Discounting

It's been said that prospects and customers don't buy based on price; they buy based on the value they receive. So this would tell you that the key to increasing price without losing customers is to show more value in what you are offering.

Small business owners often discount their prices because they think it will increase sales. But they don't realize they are destroying their profit margins when they take this approach. Discounting can, indeed, increase sales, but the additional sales often fail to cover the lost profit.

Say you discount your price by 10 percent. I'm going to show you that you will now have to sell 50 percent more products just to break even.

You sell dog toys for $100 each, with a profit margin of 30 percent, which means that you make $30 on every toy you sell. Assume your COGS for that dog toy is $70. If you discount that dog toy by 10 percent, you sell it for $90 versus $100. That brings your profit to $20 instead of $30 because your COGS are still $70.

If you sell 100 dog toys at your original profit of $30, you make $3,000. But you would have to sell 150 dog toys at your discounted price of $20 to earn $3,000. For a 10 percent discount, you now have to sell 50 percent more products to break even, let alone make a profit. The worst part is that businesses think that offering bigger discounts, such as 25 percent, will bring in more sales, but their margins inevitably take a hit.

You might say that larger companies do this all the time. That's because as companies grow larger and produce more, they often get better at it. They can buy raw materials in bulk at a discount, distribute the fixed costs of production (like machinery or buildings) across more units, and find efficiencies in their manufacturing process. All these factors can lower the cost of producing each unit, allowing the company to sell at a lower price without hurting their margins as much. And because of their strong brand recognition and loyalty, when they lower prices, they might see a more significant increase in sales volume than a smaller, less well-known company would. The key is finding the optimal balance for your specific business.

On the flip side, by increasing the price of your dog toy by a mere 10 percent and selling it for $110, you will now be making $40 in profit instead of $30, because your COGS is still $70. That's a huge 33 percent increase in profit with just a 10 percent price increase.

The key here is to innovate so that you offer more value than your competition, even if that means increasing your prices to reflect the true value of your product or service. In my business, my competitor was consistently undercutting my price. I decided that it was more important to provide prompt, quality service and keep my pricing higher. By doing that, I was able to attract better clients and get rid of the ones that only hired based on the lowest price.

Too Much Inventory

Having excess inventory will also hurt your margins. If you are overproducing and sales are not materializing as you anticipated, you will end up with excess inventory. When COGS are increased and revenue remains the same, net profit tanks.

Stop production until you can find other channels to distribute your product. Organize your stockroom and storage areas so your inventory is current and easily accessible. Clean out anything outdated or obsolete.

If you have excess inventory, determine whether it can be repurposed or sold. Try to find some way to turn it into revenue. Look for buyers who are interested in a bulk discount. If your excess inventory is unsellable, donate it to charity and claim a tax deduction.

Supplier Price Increases

One of the fastest ways for expenses to get out of hand is not having multiple suppliers or subcontractors to choose from. When you must rely on one supplier, the chances of being overcharged or paying a premium are high.

During the pandemic, I was forced to rely on one subcontractor to complete the demolition of a house I was flipping. He knew I didn't have any other options, so he started taking a longer time to complete the work, which ended up costing me more. Supply chain issues caused the cost of lumber, drywall, and other material to go through the roof. I was forced to bite the bullet and pay a premium to prevent the job from being delayed.

One company I worked with had the foresight to stock up on inventory before the global supply chain crisis hit. They took a gamble, purchased a huge amount of material, and were lucky enough to have a large warehouse to store everything. A sudden drop in inventory along with a price increase can put a business between a rock and a hard place. Many companies that weren't prepared or couldn't afford to buy and store inventory went out of business during the pandemic. This one thrived.

Always negotiate and ask for bulk discounts or substitute lower-cost materials when possible. Get new quotes from the competition, and go back to your current supplier to see if it will match the new quotes. Look for bargains, for instance, from a supplier who may need to dump inventory due to a company going out of business.

Remember to monitor your supplier invoices and take note if you see small, incremental increases. Even 2 percent or 3 percent increases can have a dramatic impact on your bottom line.

On-Demand Manufacturing

On-demand manufacturing is a method of producing goods only when you need them versus stocking up on inventory. This eliminates the need to store and manage that inventory. It will also prevent the overproduction of materials. When items aren't utilized, they often end up in landfills as waste, especially in industries like fashion, where styles come and go rapidly.

Using on-demand manufacturing will help you streamline operations as you outsource supply chain solutions. You will have time to focus on your business and what you do best. Other benefits include elevated productivity, enhanced supplier relations, and continuous quality improvement.

Bundle To Eliminate Waste

Bundling is a great marketing strategy when you want to create additional value for your business. Grouping several products or services and selling them as a single unit for one price can generate new customers. There is an appeal to the customer because they think they will save money, but they are actually spending more.

Bundling will also help you reduce inventory and move dead stock by pairing your weaker items with stronger-selling items.

Improve Quality Control

Claims, returns, and warranties need to be carefully tracked. If you constantly have to replace or fix defective products, you are losing money. Whatever the reason may be, you need to find the culprit before it affects your bottom line.

Create a quality control process to prevent your claims and returns rates from getting out of hand. Evaluate whether it's an employee problem or one caused by the material you are getting from a supplier. Whatever it is, you will need to track your processes so you can uncover the cause of the disconnect. Don't make the mistake of ignoring defects or customer complaints. Get to the bottom of it. If you find out the problem is with the wholesaler or manufacturer, make sure you address it immediately. And if the supplier isn't willing to resolve the matter, look for alternate suppliers.

Drop-Shipping

Drop-shipping is a fast-growing trend that allows business owners to sell products that are manufactured, warehoused, and shipped by third-party fulfillment companies. This method allows a lot of flexibility for businesses growing really fast or just starting out. It can lower costs associated with inventory management and help with scalability.

Although drop-shipping can provide businesses with an efficient and cost-effective way to manage inventory and grow operations, you can lose oversight of quality control and processes when a third-party handles your operations.

Chapter 4

COSTS

"Charlie (Munger) and I have not learned how to solve challenging business problems. What we have learned is to avoid them. We have done better by avoiding dragons than by slaying them." —Warren Buffett[7]

Someone once told me that in business, you are either growing or dying. There's no such thing as stagnating. If you are stagnating, it's time to make some drastic changes. In particular, it's time to get a grip on your expenses.

It's the little things that often turn into big things. All those supplies and materials you purchase daily, weekly, monthly, or annually can grow into large line items on your P&L and severely reduce your profit. In this chapter, I'll show you multiple ways to lower your overhead, including:

- Negotiate with vendors and suppliers.
- Audit software subscriptions.
- Negotiate maintenance contracts.
- Automate and outsource.
- Tap into the gig economy.
- Refinance debt.
- Evaluate your marketing strategy.
- Invest in the culture to reduce turnover.

---

7 Catherine Clifford, 5 Timeless lessons for success from the early years of Warren Buffett's annual shareholder letters, Make it, Jul, 1, 2019.

Cutting Versus Slashing

The true bottom line is that you can't slash your way to profitability. Invest in things that continue to drive revenue so that you aren't starving the resources essential to build growth and profitability. Here are a few ideas to jump-start a budget and cut unnecessary costs:

- Review financial statements often.
- Create simple systems and processes.
- Look at credit card expenses.
- Evaluate the company's goals and priorities.
- Conduct a productivity review.
- Know your marketing ROI.
- Invest in a strategic partner instead of slashing costs.

There were times when I couldn't bear to look at my company's financials. I knew we were in bad shape and didn't want to see the facts. Once I sat down and took a hard look, though, it often wasn't as bad as I imagined. Review your financials regularly and look for trends. Find ways to reduce costs and take immediate action. Develop a budget and create a more realistic forecast.

Since I started out, innovative business technology has helped to accelerate processes and tasks. Before QuickBooks became available, I used to do payroll manually, using a general ledger notepad, a No. 3 pencil, and a big eraser. Now that everything is automated, the time it takes to complete these kinds of assignments can be significantly reduced, and that helps the bottom line. Cut labor costs in other areas by using recruiting software, and implementing learning management systems, database management, and automated scheduling.

Technology has had a major, usually positive impact on the way we do business. Still, I've seen situations where a company uses technology excessively and that creates work and confusion.

Regularly evaluate your systems and processes to ensure you aren't making things more complicated than they should be.

Credit Card Expenses

Looking at your recurring credit card charges is the easiest place to find low-hanging fruit. Having a budget in place is essential, as is consistently reevaluating whether any of the costs you incur are unnecessary. Ask yourself whether your expenses will help or hurt your financial goals?

Negotiate with Vendors and Suppliers

Set aside at least a couple of hours of uninterrupted time to review bank statements, credit card statements, and vendor invoices. Audit your business and scrutinize everything with a fine-tooth comb. Decide whether the expense helps you find, get, or keep a customer. If it doesn't, eliminate it.

Review charges for your phone, internet, insurance, repairs, maintenance plans, and office supplies. There's a good chance you can do away with some of the fluff you find there. Make a note of those vendors or suppliers you could negotiate with to get a better deal or find a better company. You can often get a lower price, and you'll never know unless you try. Please don't make the mistake of getting stuck in long-term contracts for services you don't understand, such as IT maintenance. Sometimes the wording is so confusing that you don't know what you are getting. Get help from an expert to help you negotiate your contracts.

Be prepared to walk away if you don't get what you want. And don't be afraid to ask for extended payment terms or discounts. Also, consider longer-term agreements with vendors you trust to lower costs.

Consider refinancing your loans to lower your payments. You could save yourself a considerable amount of interest by consolidating debt. Talk to different bankers and make connections with people who are interested in supporting you.

Another way to reduce overhead costs is to get rid of unnecessary subscriptions. I knew a small business owner who was using twelve different apps and software that weren't integrated (the data wasn't synchronized) and didn't play well together. They weren't being utilized as intended, which caused a lot of headaches and wasted time.

In short, to keep your business expenses under control and maximize profits, regularly review and scrutinize your bank statements, credit card statements, and vendor invoices, as well as negotiate with vendors and consider consolidating loans to lower monthly payments. This will also help you stay on top of fluctuating cash flow.

If the thought of this makes you yawn, guess what? That's life. Motivate yourself with a reward afterward. Picture yourself on your porch clinking glasses with your special person and high-fiving each other for a job well done.

Know Your Marketing ROI

Small business owners typically don't have a large budget for marketing. Marketing can cost a fair bit without producing immediate results. But if you have a marketing budget, you want to ensure that you are getting the best possible results for the time and money you are investing.

Before you jump into a publicity campaign, make sure to research and create strategies. For instance, evaluate what your competitors are doing, how much you spend on customer acquisition, the uniqueness of what you offer (your differentiator), and whether you have evergreen potential.

If you are just launching a small business, the main thing you need to focus on is revenue. How many leads or contracts are you getting per day, week, or month?

Another way to judge how your business is doing is to ask the customer. Send out a survey or questionnaire. Are you providing what you think your customer will want or are you giving them what they need?

A vast number of business owners advertise online without a clue about whether they are getting results. These ads aren't cheap, and businesses often don't know whether they are leading to anything. The costs barely come close to breaking even, let alone making a profit. The data is the driver and justifies the amount spent on marketing. Any time you launch a campaign, you must identify and track key performance indicators (KPIs), a list of which you can found in the Appendix). You'll need to track how much traffic is generated, how many leads have increased, how many leads convert to customers, and how much these customers are spending.

Many people think marketing is a good way to increase revenue and profitability. The reality is some marketing campaigns generate results almost immediately, while others take weeks or even months to show a significant impact. That's because the time it takes for a marketing campaign to produce outcomes can vary widely depending on several factors, including the target audience, the type of marketing channels used, and the budget allocated.

For example, a paid search campaign or social media advertising campaign may start generating results within a few days or weeks, while a content marketing campaign or SEO strategy may take several months before showing significant results. Ultimately, the length of time it takes to see results will depend on the specific circumstances of your campaign.

Check out "The Best Marketing Bang for Your Buck" in the Appendix, where we explore two different marketing plans. The analysis will show you how spending more on marketing doesn't always equal better results.

Chapter 5
CAPACITY

"True genius resides in the capacity for evaluation of uncertain, hazardous, and conflicting information." —Winston Churchill[8]

Knowing the capacity of your workforce, product, and equipment is important for several reasons. First, it can help you plan for future growth and expansion. By understanding how much your business is capable of producing or handling, you can set realistic goals for expansion and make informed decisions about when and how to increase capacity.

Second, knowing your capacity can help you better manage your resources and allocate them efficiently. If you have an understanding of how much your business is capable of producing or handling, you can make sure that you have the right resources in place to meet demand without overloading your systems.

Third, knowing your capacity can improve your operations and identify bottlenecks or inefficiencies. By understanding where your limitations are, you can take steps to address them and increase overall efficiency and productivity.

---

8 https://en.wikipedia.org/wiki/Winston_Churchill.

Invest In Culture, Reduce Turnover

Besides getting in the habit of cutting what doesn't yield results, you will need to be proactive and invest in a few things to prevent loss. One of those things is culture.

Although we will talk about this in more detail in Chapter 11, a positive company culture can set you miles apart from your competition and will be a key factor in attracting and retaining top talent. But how do you build culture? You first have to know what culture is and what it isn't. It is not about shiny perks and unlimited personal time. These things may be part of your culture, but it goes deeper.

These are signs that a company has a great culture:

- Clear mission and values
- Transparency
- Diversity
- Long-term employees
- Comfortable atmosphere
- Absence of office politics
- Wins are celebrated.
- Leaders are visible and accessible.
- Teams are involved in the company's success.
- Employees are more than just colleagues, they are friends.
- There are ongoing professional development opportunities.

Automation Versus Outsourcing

Automation is a way to streamline a process. Outsourcing is having an outside firm or person conduct the work. If you one of your goals is to increase efficiency and capacity while reducing costs, include automation and outsourcing in your plan.

There are easy ways to set up automation in a small company to do things like email campaigns, creating standard operating procedures (SOPs), uploading all your client contact information to a centralized database or CRM, social media scheduling, text messaging to respond to customer service requests and a lead scoring system.

You can easily find highly qualified professionals both onshore and offshore to outsource the work that you do. Many business owners I know have an offshore VA (virtual assistant). Other tasks, such as accounting, bookkeeping, and IT, can also be outsourced for substantial savings. A major advantage to outsourcing is that you can designate the worker as 1099, which can save you a ton when it comes to perks and benefits such as health care, retirement funds, and payroll taxes. Outsourcing is worth considering if your business is struggling and looking for a short-term fix.

Tap into the Gig Economy

After COVID-19 struck, many small business owners found themselves in a bind. In particular, they battled labor shortages and inflation in the wake of a tsunami of resignations, a period now known as the Great Resignation. Suddenly, there was a significant imbalance between worker supply and employer demand. Positions that had been easy to fill were now all but impossible to fill.

During COVID, millions got sick or lost their jobs, or both, and they were forced to isolate at home for months. Many reconsidered their options, discovered they loved the freedom of working from home, and took advantage of the gig economy. Some eventually returned to work; a wealth of talented workers continued to freelance. If you are having trouble filling a position, check out some well-known gig sites, such as Upwork, Freelancer, TaskRabbit, and Fiverr.

Goals and Priorities

What are your goals? Where do you want to be in three, five, or ten years? As a leader, it's up to you to clearly identify the goals and priorities that will set the tone for the whole company. Once this is done, you can easily distinguish between the must-haves and the nice-to-haves. Your responsibility is to measure each expenditure against how the organization will meet and exceed its goals. Make sure you prioritize the most important actions that will support you in this process.

Conduct a Productivity Review

Do you know what your staff is doing? Do you know your cost of doing business by the week, the day, or the hour?

For a productivity review start by assessing the workload. Divide your employees into direct versus indirect, salaried versus hourly, and whatever is relevant to your business. Review billable and non-billable positions (if applicable), and determine which employees are consistently profitable. Are they are doing something different from the rest? How can you re-create their success?

Ask employees to write down what they do daily, weekly, and monthly. This will look like their job description, laying out their roles and responsibilities; it will become an accountability document with metrics in place to measure their progress. Review the document with them and look for any duplications. Are they doing anything that someone else is accountable for or tasks that should be eliminated or delegated to someone else? Be thorough. Ask if they forgot to list anything?

This process will greatly improve business productivity, especially if everyone is now focused on the highest impact-producing activities. This approach can lead to a big reduction in overtime costs, too.

Invest in a Strategic Partner

When I started my business, I hired people smarter than me. I was lucky enough to have grown up in an entrepreneurial family and came in with many lessons already learned. I knew if I surrounded myself with reliable experts, they would teach me what I needed to know. I would have the same accountant, banker, and attorney for years to come.

Seek advice from people who can give you an outside perspective. Work with a business adviser, especially one who has had the practical experience of owning their own business. That person can help you put together a solid strategic growth and business plan to focus on outcomes and goals. They will also hold you accountable and identify any bad habits or patterns you have developed, such as being overreactive and prone to excessive hiring and firing. Working with an adviser who establishes a working partnership with you can make all the difference in the world.

Next, we'll turn to another key aspect of your business—knowing what's coming around the bend—and forecasting the future using both historical data and a little gut instinct.

Chapter 6

CRYSTAL BALLS

"I skate to where the puck is going to be, not where it has been."
—*Wayne Gretzky*[9]

In this chapter, we will discuss more ways to optimize your business. Whenever you wonder if it's the right time to hire someone or buy that new piece of equipment, this is where budgeting, forecasting, pro formats, and projections come into play. These terms are often used interchangeably, but they are not the same. Let's break them down.

A budget is where you want the business to go. A forecast is where the company is headed. A projection is hypothetical and based on some type of addition or event. Pro formas are historical statements adjusted for the effects of a future transaction. Confused yet?

Then there is benchmarking, a tool to help you see where you stand in relation to other businesses in the same industry. Benchmarking is not to be confused with a balanced scorecard, since they are two different initiatives. A balanced scorecard is used to keep track of the execution of activities and to monitor results. Whereas KPIs are used to measure performance, scorecards display the success or failure of those efforts to reach a goal.

---

9 Houston Mitchell, Steve Jobs Used Wayne Gretzky as inspiration, Los Angeles Times, Oct. 6, 2011. https://www.latimes.com/archives/blogs/sports-now/story/2011-10-06/steve-jobs-used-wayne-gretzky-as-inspiration.

Some of the predictive tools are a little bit art and a little bit science. They are your crystal ball of assumptions and historical data. Projections and presumptions show how a company can improve its financial situation if a beneficial change occurs. But mostly, it's all fortune-telling. That's how business works. You set goals and do what you can to reach them, but sometimes you have to pivot based on predictions, forecasts, trends, or a new reality.

Benchmarking

One of the key questions you need to answer is whether your business is trending compared to your competitors and industry leaders. To keep it simple, let's say you are in one of the following three categories: the good, the bad, or the ugly.

The "good" category would be considered above average, and the "bad" would be below average. If you're having consistent financial and operational problems in your business, there's a decent chance you're in the "ugly" group. No judgment here. It's not a death sentence. There are ways you can recover—remember the several approaches we've discussed to increase revenue and lower COGS and overhead without spending a dime.

Once you determine where your business falls compared to other companies in your industry, you can identify internal improvement opportunities and unlock your hidden growth potential. These might include setting performance expectations, improving services or the quality of products, or using pricing tier strategies.

Forecasting

The forecast will tell you where the business is going. It's an estimation of what it will take to fund future operations. It will help you make key decisions based on past events, as well as anticipate future trends.

Your priority is establishing a baseline by looking at your historical data. You can either do a long-term or short-term forecast. Here are the steps:

- List the various revenue streams for the goods or services you sell.
- Estimate how much you expect to sell over the coming months.
- Define the dollar amount of each product or service.
- Determine your COGS (what it will cost to produce and sell each good or service you provide).

Seasonality

Seasonality is useful for identifying seasonal effects on sales and predicting patterns in future business activity. Staying on top of your fluctuating business sales is crucial for planning because it can have a huge impact on your cash flow. This is especially true if you own a seasonal or cyclical business.

Monthly Revenue ÷ Annual Revenue = Seasonal Effects

July	Aug.	Sept.	Oct.	Nov.	Dec.	Total
5.50%	6.25%	10.00%	15.00%	19.50%	23.00%	100.00%
$22,000	$25,000	$40,000	$60,000	$78,000	$92,000	$400,000

Table 6.1. A snapshot of the second half of the year for DogToyz. The holiday season brings in the majority of annual revenue.

Pro Forma

A pro forma financial statement is an analysis based on financial assumptions or projections, and, as such, it is also known as a cash flow projection. Pro formas are historical statements adjusted for the effects of a future transaction and are typically generated to represent cash flow over multiple years. An excellent example of when you need a pro forma is when one business is considering acquiring another company and is seeking finance for this purpose.

Let's break down how to put together a pro forma statement in three manageable steps.

1. Estimate the amount of income you will get monthly. Adjust the amounts either higher or lower, depending on outside factors such as weather or seasonality, which will affect sales.

2. Estimate the expenses you'll have, based on historical data.

3. Review each column and the numbers you entered. These will tell you how much you need to sell or the value of new contracts you need to get in order to achieve the revenue numbers. Revise and tweak until the numbers make sense for your business and they give you a bigger picture of what needs to happen to hit your goals.

Profitability

We have already talked about how revenue, COGS, and overhead are the three numbers to focus on in order to generate more profit. But let's dive in a little deeper to see how to use those numbers to generate additional results.

Suppose your business generated 1,200 leads in the past year by getting 100 new leads per month. If your average conversion rate was 20 percent, you had 240 annual sales. Let's also say that your 240 customers each purchased your product twelve times from you throughout the year and paid an average of $100 per purchase. That's $288,000 in revenue from those new customers during the year.

If your profit margin per sale is 20 percent, you will earn $57,600 annually. If you were to increase five areas (leads, conversions, transactions, prices, gross profits) by 10 percent, you'd see your profit almost double.

A 10 percent gain in these five areas is decent. But what if you raised it more? The third column shows what happens when you increase each of the five areas by 50 percent. Your profit goes from $57,600 to nearly half a million dollars annually. That's a 791 percent increase! You can completely transform your business by increasing leads, conversions, sales, and transactions. These simple calculations show it's possible.

Description	Baseline	+10%	+50%
Number of leads	1,200	1,320	1,800
Conversions	20%	30%	40%
Sales	240	396	720
Transactions	12	13	18
Price	100	110	150
Revenue	288,000	433,290	1,520,100
Gross Profit	57,600	933,324	456,030
Gross Profit %	20%	22%	30%

Table 6.2: Transform your business by increasing leads, conversions, sales, and transactions.

Three Buckets

Creating a three-bucket strategy can be a helpful exercise to avoid unnecessary risks. Some companies find themselves in a situation where they are relying on one or two customers to provide 100 percent of their sales. This can be a risky position for a lot of reasons, mainly because you are one decision away from disaster. It can also be just as bad to have a ton of small customers that are not your ideal client. These are the ones that are slow paying, have unrealistic expectations, or complain about everything.

Let's say you have 1,000 customers, of which 948 purchase $500 worth of dog toys a month. You have 50 customers that purchase $5,000 in dog toys per month, and two large customers that purchase 50,000 dog toys per month for a total of $824,000 in monthly sales. If we put them in categories of low, medium, and high, we come up with percentages of sales as follows:

Low	Medium	High
948 @ $500 = $474,000 58% of sales	50 @ $5,000 = $250,000 30% of sales	2 @ $50,000 = $100,000 12% of sales

Table 6.3: Spread of sales with 1,000 customers, most making small purchases.

Look what happens when you let go of some of your less-desirable customers and focus on getting more premier clients that will pay for middle and high-end ticket items. Your sales increase by nearly 50 percent, going from $841,000 to $1.7 million, with 25 percent fewer clients.

Low	Medium	High
500 @ $500 = $250,000 15% of sales	250 @ $5,000 = $1,250,000 73% of sales	4 @ $50,000 = $200,000 12% of sales

Table 6.4: Sales with more premier clients buying more big-ticket items, fewer less-desirable clients, produces higher profits.

By increasing the number of sales on your bigger ticket items, you can potentially offset the cost of goods sold and make a higher gross margin, which allows more sales to flow through as profit.

To build a successful and sustainable business, it's important to have a strong understanding of your cash flow, capital, costs, and capacity. By focusing on increasing revenue, reducing costs of goods sold and overhead, and optimizing collections and accounts receivable, you can improve your profitability and maximize your resources. It's also crucial to keep a close eye on pricing and to continuously evaluate and adjust your strategy based on market trends and demand.

In addition, investing in culture and productivity, leveraging automation and outsourcing, and building strategic partnerships can help you scale your operations and drive top-line growth. And finally, while you can't predict the future with certainty, by benchmarking, forecasting, and using tools like pro forma financial statements, you can make informed decisions and navigate changes with confidence.

Increasing sales on bigger-ticket items can have a significant impact on your bottom line. However, to build a successful and sustainable business, you must have a deep understanding of your financials and focus on revenue growth, cost reduction, and productivity optimization. By investing in culture, leveraging technology, building partnerships, and using forecasting tools, you can stay ahead of market trends and navigate changes with confidence.

Congrats! You did it. You made it through the math and the business lingo. Now that you have a handle on the nitty-gritty of launching and running the lucrative business of your dreams, let's turn to the equally important second half of the pie: the secrets of successful leadership.

PART TWO

Carve a Middle Way Path to Leadership Mastery

Chapter 7
TWELVE PRINCIPLES

"Within every adversity is the seed of an equal or greater benefit. Within every problem is an opportunity. Even in the knocks of life, we can find great gifts." —Napoleon Hill[10]

There is a story about three great leaders who met to discuss the world's problems. They sat down for a cup of tea, but the devious servant poured them vinegar instead.

The first leader, Confucius, took a sip of his tea and said it tasted sour. He talked about how the world is full of degenerate people who lacked virtues and a moral outlook. The second leader, Buddha sipped his tea and said he found the taste to be bitter. He talked about how life is suffering, and people could end their suffering if they let go of their attachment to desire. The third leader, Lao Tzu took a long sip. He smiled and said he found the tea to be sweet. He talked about how judgment is our folly. The great way is effortless, but people go against nature and deviate from the path that will make them the most content.

The Middle Way

Lao Tzu was the founder of Taoism, and the Middle Way is a key principle in Taoist philosophy that refers to a path of balance by avoiding

---

10 Napoleon Hill, Think and Grow Rich: Original Classic Edition, G&D Media, 2019.

extremes.

In this sense, the desirable middle is similar to Aristotle's Golden Mean, which refers to the virtue of moderation between the two extremes of excess and deficiency.

The Middle Way is to live in accordance with the natural flow of the universe rather than trying to control or manipulate it. This will lead to a more fulfilling, peaceful life through daily actions of simplicity, patience, and compassion. Embracing the Middle Way, learning to let go of controlling outcomes, accepting what is, and going with the flow, is something I abide by both in life and in business, which has led me to greater fulfillment and joy.

I've found that there are twelve principles of business and leadership that, if followed, will never lead you astray. If you can find big and small ways to integrate these into daily operations, you will find yourself farther down the path to success before you know it.

Grab your notebook, rank your strengths and weaknesses from the list, and jot down ways to incorporate them into your day-to-day business operations.

Twelve Principles of Middle Way Leadership

1. **The Principle of Cash (Profitability).** Stay on the path of growth. It can be easy to make money but hard to make a profit. Cash is a tool to build the business you envision. A Middle Way leader encourages resourcefulness, strives for continuous improvement, and focuses on profitability. Trusting your instinct is good as long as you have the facts to back up your decisions.

2. **The Principle of Control.** Train and discipline the mind to be aware of unknown blind spots that can hold you back. Embrace the reality of issues as they are, and work with what you have. Middle Way leaders are conscientious, develop a deep awareness, and know when to take control and when to let go.

3. **The Principle of Courage.** Courage takes effort. You must be willing to face your fears, knowing you may fail but choosing to take the risk and forge ahead anyway. The Middle Way leader develops the good in others, establishes direction, and leads their team toward actionable steps.

4. **The Principle of Creativity.** Be mindful to never lose your power to develop an evolving vision. Challenge your-self to adopt a compassionate perspective and create a safe environment that encourages your team and spurs their innovation. Middle Way leaders create a new or better way to build, sell, or develop, and turn ideas into actions.

5. **The Principle of Culture.** There is honor and value in running a business that enhances people's well-being and quality of life. Middle Way leaders celebrate diversity and inclusivity of thought, opinion, skills and competencies to foster success and drive organizational impact.

6. **The Principle of Collaboration.** Build high-functioning teams, partnerships, and associations by maximizing strengths and minimizing weaknesses to lead to a balanced course of initiatives. A Middle Way leader knows how to work with different personalities, gets everyone's buy-in, and builds excitement toward future objectives.

7. **The Principle of Conflict.** Conflict is good if it's healthy and solution oriented. Being vulnerable and letting go of assumptions and biases can create opportunities for growth and can improve self-awareness. Middle Way leaders arm themselves with dignity, maintain personal integrity, and pick their battles wisely.

8. **The Principle of Communication.** Being intentional about transferring information within and outside the business requires understanding the power of words, knowing when to speak, and when to listen. A Middle Way leader easily communicates expectations, builds strong relationships, and successfully delegates tasks.

9. **The Principle of Competition.** Evaluate whether being the first and the fastest is the best. Sometimes slow and steady wins the race. Seeking reward and surpassing rivals is best when guided by ethical and moral codes grounded

in harmony for the greater good. A Middle Way leader is honorable and does no harm.

10. **The Principle of Choices.** Know how to choose the right action when there are several options to pick from. Middle Way leaders are aware of why they do what they do, understanding all the potential consequences that will result from the decisions they make.

11. **The Principle of Change.** Change is a journey with many steps. Encouraging resourcefulness and striving for continuous improvement one step at a time is the best path to take. You can't change the world, but you can change how you look at the world.

12. **The Principle of Compliance.** Upholding the ethics that govern your business and industry is crucial to maintaining trust and credibility. Compliance is not merely a checkbox but a commitment that embodies a deep respect for integrity, fairness, and transparency. Middle Way leaders make it a priority to align with values that drive sustainable success.

As you read on, I'll guide you through how to integrate each of these principles into your day-to-day operations, find balance in the chaos of running a company, enhance your leadership skills, and take your business to the next level.

Chapter 8
CONTROL

"There is a force in the universe that makes things happen and all you have to do is get in touch with it. Stop thinking, let things happen, and be the ball."—Chevy Chase, Caddyshack[11]

What is leadership? The title CEO, for instance, does not a leader make without the willingness to accept the responsibility for the whole. Are leaders born or made? What makes people follow someone? One thing is sure: It's easy to recognize a lousy leader.

A Title Does Not a Leader Make

It has been said that there are essential components to being a good leader, things like competency, commitment, character, confidence, and candor. When I started out, I didn't have a clue what being a leader required. All I had was courage, the kind of courage that comes with having nothing to lose.

President Harry S. Truman's definition of a leader was a man "who can persuade people to do what they don't want to do, or do what they're too lazy to do and like it." That traditional, authoritarian approach may have gotten us through the Industrial Age, but things have changed.

---

11 https://www.imdb.com/title/tt0080487/characters/nm0000331.

I would say that a leader is someone who can motivate and influence a person or group of people to achieve a goal.

There are many different types of leaders. Here are a few of my favorites:

- **The Founder.** Hands-on, learns by doing, their dream is to sell the company in two years for a gazillion dollars, until they come to grips with reality.

- **The Solopreneur.** Comfortable lifestyle brand, not interested in scale, enjoys the privilege of being recognized as a business owner.

- **The Wantrepreneur.** A massive dreamer who wants to change the world but is afraid to go for it.

- **The Ambassador.** A professional, entrusted with the position, and responsible for representing the organization and promoting its interests.

- **The Creator.** A great delegator, has long-term goals, is interested in job creation.

- **The Analyst.** The turnaround expert, lives by the dashboard, and knows how to grow by cutting the fat.

For CEOs, there are really two categories. The first exudes confidence, has a big picture, long-term vision, and knows how to set and achieve smart goals. They stand up to the scrutiny of tough decisions because they have the courage to fail. Where intelligence is one part of the equation, fearlessness can be a path to success. I'll call these the innovators.

The other type, the implementers, are less strategic and more hands-on, more tactical. They produce results by building processes and tracking progress with metrics dashboards and performance management, and by analyzing and tweaking their accountability. But when up against the wall and forced to make a decision, they tend to waffle.

Even though being a successful CEO requires skills from both categories, most tend to be more comfortable with one style or the other. Innovators are happily setting the direction and vision of the company, and implementers know how to make a company run well. Typically, but not always, innovators run the company with a team of implementers. Although both can be good CEOs, you need a blend of the two to be a great CEO.

Meanwhile, if you share the title of CEO with a fifty-fifty partner, it's vital to create clearly defined roles and responsibilities. Identify which person will generally take the lead and plan to present a unified front. Or, if you truly want to split duties evenly, make sure your organization is set up in such a way that things are not commingled or confusing.

If you skip this step, your employees may suffer from "double approval" syndrome, which can send them in circles. It also leads to the "ask mom or dad until you get the answer you want" game. No matter what, there's a loss of decision-making efficiency. Everything becomes a bottleneck, and you begin to experience slow and unwieldy growth. Somebody must have the final say. Somebody must be in charge. Someone must be able to make decisions quickly with limited information.

That is a leader.

Before we dive in, let's review some terminology that we'll return to throughout the book. Whatever your natural approach to leadership, you can be trained in many styles.

The most effective style for a particular leader depends on a variety of factors, such as overall goals and the leader's and team's personality and preferences.

Here are some common leadership styles:

- **Autocratic.** This leader makes decisions without consulting anyone and expects everyone to follow orders. This style is effective when immediate action is needed. Still, it may stifle creativity or engagement.

- **Democratic.** This style is characterized by a leader who involves team members in decision-making and encourages them to participate in the process. This fosters a sense of ownership and commitment among team members but could slow down decision-making.

- **Laissez-faire.** This type of leader gives people a high degree of freedom and autonomy to make their own decisions and solve problems. This style empowers and fosters creativity. Still, it may be less effective in ensuring that work is completed on time and to a high standard.

- **Transformational.** This is the leader who motivates people to achieve their full potential and make a positive impact. They have a clear vision for the future and inspire others to work towards that vision.

- **Servant.** This leader puts the needs of their team or organization before their own. They are focused on empowering and developing their team. Servant leaders prioritize collaboration and communication, which results in a positive work culture.

According to situational leadership theory, the most effective style for a particular leader will depend on the competence and commitment of their team members. Leaders are encouraged to assess the needs and abilities of their team and adjust their style accordingly to achieve the best results.

Here are the four basic situational leadership styles[12]:

- **Telling.** The leader provides clear direction and guidance and expects team members to follow orders. This style is appropriate when team members have low competence and low commitment.

- **Selling.** The leader provides more direction and guidance, encourages team members to participate in the decision-making process, and provides support and resources. This style is appropriate when team members have low competence but high commitment.

- **Participating.** The leader involves team members in decision-making and encourages collaboration but still provides some guidance and direction. This style is appropriate when team members have moderate competence and commitment.

- **Delegating.** The leader gives team members a high degree of autonomy and trusts them to make their own decisions. This style is appropriate when team members have high competence and commitment.

The emotional component of situational leadership styles involves the leader's ability to assess not only the competence and commitment of their team members but also their emotional states, such as their level of confidence or motivation so the leader can adapt accordingly.

Daniel Goleman, Richard Boyatzis, and Annie McKee[13]—all experts in emotional intelligence—have developed a theory called primal leadership based on the idea that emotions play a crucial role in how people think, act, and behave. According to the theory, leaders who create a positive emotional climate foster a sense of connection

---

12 Dr. Paul Hersey, *The Situational Leader*, Warner Books, 1986.
13 Daniel Goleman, Richard E. Boyatzis, Annie McKee, *Primal Leadership, Unleashing the Power of Emotional Intelligence*, Harvard Business Review Press, 2013. https://hbr.org/2001/12/primal-leadership-the-hidden-driver-of-great-performance.

and commitment among their team members, leading to increased collaboration, creativity, and productivity, and improved performance and outcomes. Research has shown the percentage of time people feel positive emotions at work is the strongest predictor of job satisfaction. Spreading good vibes and positive emotions will drive your business toward success.

Influential primal leaders—especially ones who incorporate an emotionally intelligent leadership style—have strong communication skills and build robust relationships with their team members. To be an effective primal leader, it is vital to be able to identify and manage your own emotions and those of your team members. This includes recognizing and addressing negative emotions, such as frustration or anger, as well as cultivating positive ones, such as gratitude and joy.

A leader can be a coach, too, in the sense of providing guidance, support, and mentorship to their team to help them develop skills and reach goals. Coaching is a leadership style that provides employees with the resources and support they need to succeed rather than simply giving them orders or directives. Effective leaders who coach often have strong communication skills and can listen actively and provide constructive feedback. (Note that not all leaders are coaches and not all coaching is done by leaders.

A professional coach can provide similar support and may work with individuals or teams to help them improve their performance or achieve specific goals. In this context, the coach may not have formal leadership roles.)

Leadership experts James M. Kouzes and Barry Z. Posner[14] have a leadership model called the Practice of Exemplary Leadership, which is

---

14 James M. Kouzes and Barry Z. Posner, *The Leadership Challenge: How to Make Extraordinary Things Happen In Organizations*, Jossey-Bass, 2023. https://www.leadershipchallenge.com/research/five-practices.aspx.

based on the idea that leadership is a practice that can be learned and developed through experience.

There are five practices that exemplary leaders engage in, according to Kouzes and Posner:

Model the way. Exemplary leaders set a good example for their team or organization by consistently acting according to their values and beliefs.

Inspire a shared vision. Exemplary leaders articulate a compelling and inspiring vision for the future and help others see how they can contribute to achieving that vision.

Challenge the process. Exemplary leaders are willing to take risks and try new approaches to achieve their goals.

Enable others to act. Exemplary leaders provide their teams with the resources, support, and opportunities they need to succeed.

Encourage the heart. Exemplary leaders recognize and appreciate the contributions of their team members and create a positive and supportive work environment.

This model is based on extensive research and has been widely adopted in business and leadership development programs. It is often used as a framework for developing leadership skills and behaviors.

A Style To Suit You

Research has shown there is no single leadership style that is better than others. In fact, there is often a mix of four or five qualities that will achieve company goals faster. Being aware of the strengths and weaknesses of each type is vital to being an effective leader. It's important to be flexible and adaptable, depending on the situation.

Here are some additional styles of leadership:

- **Transformational.** Gives opportunities to explore different approaches and ideas.

- **Delegative.** Gives little guidance, with lots of freedom for others to make decisions.

- **Authoritative.** Commands and controls by setting procedures.

- **Transactional.** Sets targets and rewards based on performance.

- **Participative.** Encourages collaboration.

- **Pacesetting.** Leads by example, "models the way."

- **Coaching.** Leads by mentoring and encourages a focus on strengths and talent.

- **Affiliative.** Leads by creating harmony.

- **Visionary/Charismatic.** Leads by inspiring.

- **Emergent.** Develops over time, based on influence rather than authority.

- **Situational.** Chooses a style based on which best fits the situation.

What defines a leader is personal and includes many variables, including the jobs we choose, the lifestyles we lead, the expectations and goals we create, and the assumptions we make. Leadership seems to come naturally for some, and for others, it's a learning process. You don't have to be born with it; it can be learned.

Great leaders have charisma, emotional intelligence, and self-awareness. They serve and inspire others to do even greater things. They challenge us and take us places we could never imagine. They take risks and take responsibility for failures. They acknowledge the contributions of others and give them credit for their successes. Leaders remain calm under pressure and listen and communicate effectively. They adapt to the circumstances, which earns them the respect they deserve.

Stupid Things Business Owners Do

Have you ever wondered why some businesses fail and others succeed, even if they provide the same product or service? Whatever their style, even the best-intentioned leaders can stumble if they fall into one of several common traps. Spending the last few years coaching business owners worldwide, I've discovered some simple signs that lead to trouble.

These are bad practices every business owner should avoid:

- **Being a slave to time bandits.** If you're always putting out fires, shooting from the hip, and being reactive instead of proactive, you're wasting money and energy. Stop getting hijacked and put an end to the interruptions. Create a time management plan and stick to it.

- **Stagnation.** Running a company into the ground doesn't take long. Stagnation is a bad sign that things are about to shift, either toward growth or failure. Act quickly to make sure it's the former. Jump to the next level by researching the competition and then look for ways to reinvent your brand, product, or service. Evolve or die.

- **Poor planning or vision.** Watch for cyclical and seasonal trends, and have safeguards in place to protect against negative internal and external events. Focus on the company's mission or have a consultant conduct a gap analysis to help see what's missing between where you are and where you want to be. Clearly defined organizational processes are the special sauce for any well-run company.

- **No sales or marketing process.** If you aren't sending the right message to the right distribution channels, you are losing money. You can't be everything to everybody. Narrow your niche, create a brand (not bland) personality, and focus on attracting the ideal client, within the right target market.

- **Bad customer service.** Losing touch with your customers is a death sentence. Social media has made it easy for disgruntled clients to badmouth you. Reach out to a dozen or so of your recent customers for a little Q&A. Ask tough questions about how your company can improve, and then take action, fast.

- **Mediocre advisers.** Are you eating with buzzards instead of flying with eagles? Don't scrimp when hiring an attorney, banker, or accountant. Surround yourself with people who are experts in their fields and easily do the tasks or activities that are not at your comfort level. Form a mastermind group of people from other industries who can provide unbiased opinions and support.

- **Being an absentee owner.** You've stuck a "gone fishing" sign on your office door and left others in charge. That's fine and, yes, necessary at times, but if you are often unavailable, you are asking for trouble. Don't think that you can slack off after you've put the right people in the right seats. You still have to drive the bus.

- **Wearing too many hats.** Entrepreneurs may feel it's easier to do everything themselves. But do you really have to do it all, or are you afraid to release some control to others? Focus at least 80 percent of your time on what you do best, which should be generating revenue. Eliminate the time you spend on minutiae by delegating, automating, or bartering services.

- **Budget? What budget?** Spending foolishly can dig a hole so quickly that you'll be lucky if you can see your way out. Do you really need that upscale office space if your customers don't visit? Do you really need to drive that expensive car? Take a gut check, drop the ego, and stop the bloodletting.

- **Mindset issues.** If you are struggling with personal issues such as fear of success or failure, low self-esteem, or poor decision-making, the business will suffer. Get unstuck, hire a coach to help you stay on track, set goals, and hold yourself accountable. Work on yourself as well as the business.

If any of the above are ringing a bell, either about you or a company you've worked for—or if you just want to make sure to avoid these pitfalls—don't despair. With my guidance, you will set yourself apart from the competition and build a conscientious and principled company.

Going from Bad Boss to Badass Boss

Along the way, I developed my own style of leadership. It often happened by trial and error—lots and lots of errors. But when I look back at all the mistakes I made, I was always learning from the failures. The most important thing was to understand myself, uncover my blind spots, and question my assumptions. Our unconscious bias can influence our decision-making, and unless we have awareness, we can make bad decisions based on our judgments and perceptions of others.

Here are the lessons that form the foundation of my thinking about positive and effective leadership:

- Know your strengths and weaknesses.
- Keep practicing and honing your skills.
- Know how to resolve or mediate conflict.

- Know when people are conflict-avoidant.
- Develop situational awareness.
- Be aware of personality types and preferences.
- Be adaptable, flexible, and bounce back from mistakes.
- Listen to understand.

Being a good leader involves authenticity and transparency. Sometimes that means doing hard things and being honest. As a CEO, this can feel unnatural. Say your friend tells you a bad joke. Your response is, "I think the punchline fell short and your delivery was dry. How about you rewrite the script and come back to me when you have something better?" Of course, your friend might tell you to eff off.

It's unnatural to evaluate and critique people's performance every day, but this is what a CEO does. In order to be effective at it and not have your employees say yes to your face but critique you behind your back, you need to develop your own style of delivery.

The old way of delivering feedback was the baloney sandwich. That's where someone compliments you, then tells you where you really screwed up, and then compliments you again. It's hug, slap, hug. That type of delivery is deceptive and doesn't feel good to the person you are saying it to. Every time you are nice in the future, they will be thinking, "Here it comes." It puts your employees on guard and erodes their trust.

Pick a way of delivering negative information in a positive way. Think about how you can match your delivery and tone to the person you are speaking to. One style that has worked for me is to evaluate objectively with a focus on future activity to get the results I want. I say, "This is what I liked about what you did, and this is what I'd recommend you try in the future."

There's no one best leadership style, and the most effective style for a particular leader may depend on the context and the needs of the team or organization.

EXERCISE: LEADERSHIP MASTERY

There are many attributes of being a great leader, but here are three that are simple, which doesn't mean easy. If you can master these qualities, your people will listen to you and want to follow where you are leading.

You must be able to:

Paint a vision of what's possible.

Build trust.

Show you have the skills and competency to accomplish your vision.

Here are other leadership skills and outcomes to consider:

- *Articulate the vision and get the buy-in* Great leaders can communicate their vision. They are dynamic and compelling, which makes people eager to follow them.

- *Align interests and people.* Leaders who are authentic and care more about their people than fame or glory build amazing teams and loyal followers.

- *Execute and achieve the vision.* This comes down to competence and skill. People want to work for leaders whom they trust can get the job done.

Now, consider your style of leadership. Set aside some time to list your qualities and strengths and what you want to aspire to, say, five years in the future.

- How will you show up?
- Will you lead with integrity, professionalism, and consistency?
- What's your vision of the best version of yourself?
- How will you move towards evolving and growing to that next level?

- How will you challenge yourself to take risks, to be open and curious?
- Will you be a "good finder" and see the best in others?
- How will you relate to people to show you have heart, passion, and conviction?
- How will you diversify or differentiate yourself from other leaders or business owners?

The positive qualities associated with leadership, such as intelligence, determination, and vision, are required for greatness, but they are insufficient. The latest research tells us that to be a great leader, one must also have strong emotional intelligence (EI) skills. The five components of EI are self-awareness, self-regulation, motivation, empathy, and the ability to maintain positive relationships. These qualities may not sound very businesslike, but there is a direct link between such soft, or interpersonal, abilities and measurable results.

A leader with high EI works well with others and is effective at leading change. They bestow credit and shoulder the blame. They make good promises. They dispel our fear when times are tough, help us navigate through uncertainty, and inspire us to tap into their undiscovered strengths, unlocking our peak potential. Attitudes and emotions are contagious. The strongest emotion in the room can ripple out and elicit the same feeling in others without anyone's conscious **awareness of what's happening.**

If you Google "the dark side of business," you get a billion results covering everything from the rise of narcissism and greed to complacency and sleazy competition tactics. The winds of fortune made fast are shifting with stories of fraud, inequality, data manipulation and tracking. People have started to question Big Tech's domination and the flip side underbelly of lousy behavior, like when one of the biggest companies in the world decided to fire its whistleblowers. But the problem doesn't just pertain to the big guys. Small companies are guilty, too.

If you want to rise above these questionable tactics to launch a company and a workplace that is inclusive and productive, there are several ways to begin integrating a conscious approach. These include:

- *Mindfulness practice.* Implement exercise programs to help employees reduce stress and increase focus and productivity.
- *Be solution-focused.* Create a more positive and collaborative work environment by switching from a focus on problems to a focus on solutions.
- *Take a values-added approach.* Emphasizing purpose and values in business can lead to a more sustainable and socially responsible company.
- *Have emotional intelligence.* Incorporate training for better communication, problem-solving, and decision-making.
- *Exhibit ethical behavior.* Encourage a culture that rewards people to act in ways that are consistent with the company's values.
- *Prefer sustainability.* Adopt operations and supply chain practices to minimize environmental impacts while promoting social and economic well-being. Essentially, this means meeting the needs of the present without compromising future generations.

EXERCISE: EIGHT QUESTIONS

Let's turn to eight leadership questions that can put you in a mindset to repair foolish mistakes, improve business success, keep ethics top of mind, and launch grander diversity and inclusion plans. Whenever I run coaching sessions, I ask the CEO and any leaders to contemplate these questions and consider how they can apply them to their company.

1. Improve mental well-being. How can we address mental health issues in the workplace to reduce heath-care costs and improve job performance, engagement, and productivity?

Psychological disorders are prevalent in the workplace. In 2021, the American Psychological Association reported nearly three in five employees (59 percent) said they have experienced negative impacts of work-related stress, and 87 percent think actions from their employer could help their mental health.

Think about it. You spend 90,000 hours at work over a lifetime, likely with coworkers suffering from one or more mental or emotional disorders. This can be a huge stressor for everyone, especially without education or preparation to help deal with it. Make it a priority to provide training or other programs to enhance your employees' mental and emotional health and wellness.

2. Focus on leadership. What needs to happen to make top-performing teams more engaged and invested in the company's growth?

There is a real lack of leadership in small businesses, especially in the tech industry. Maybe this stems from avoiding adversity, whether intentionally or not (see number 6 below). I've witnessed founders with so little talent for leadership that they can't make decisions, flounder, and fail to execute. Many don't have the skills and mindset needed to build high-performing teams because they are too busy thinking about what they need or are too focused on product-related problems they believe are more critical. A good leader requires insight, awareness, and the ability to keep a pulse on every aspect of the company.

3. Invest in employees. Invest in the development of each individual. Ask how you can prepare for rapid growth and invest in and support staff to help them get ready for more significant roles and responsibilities?

Some companies pour money into things that don't result in a return. While a company may be focused on investing in creating a successful image, neglecting to invest in its employees can result in financial loss. Employee development is not an expense; it's an investment. The well-trained employee is loyal, does better work, will help you build a better reputation, and will save you more time, money, and headaches in the long run. Think of a good employee strategically. The investment pays off every month.

4. Pay attention to the small stuff. How can we help the team cope with high expectations without falling into unhealthy and toxic behaviors?

We've all heard of companies that face allegations of toxic work culture or misogynistic behavior. Bad behavior often starts slow as people test how far they can push boundaries. One nasty comment or overlooked action can activate a chain reaction and cause a shift in related behaviors. If left unchecked by leadership, the toxicity invades all aspects of the organization. It doesn't help that the traditional hierarchy makes employees feel as though they are mere peasants without power.

People are motivated by different things. Some will put up with a ton of bad behavior because they live paycheck to paycheck. Others get status and power by being aligned with the company and are too afraid to speak up or rock the boat. Develop steps to counter toxic behavior. Seek regular feedback from your staff. Lead by example, set clear guidelines, honor cultural differences, and uncover shared values.

5. Make integrity a priority. How can we maintain integrity, convey greater authenticity, and build trust with investors, vendors, and clients?

Believing in your dream is important but not as crucial as being in touch with reality. I've witnessed founders get so caught up in inflated forecasts and selling their pitch that they cross the line between honesty and fantasy. It's like exaggerating on your resume but with much higher stakes. Misleading investors is a level of deception that will come back to bite you. If you can't be trusted to know your numbers, how can you be trusted with anything else in the business?

6. Focus on the big picture. How is the company articulating a clear and compelling vision for the greater mission and purpose to be quickly adopted by everyone involved?

Once, I spent eighteen long months developing a prototype. It was an interactive game to teach kids ages eight to twelve how to build healthy coping mechanisms, such as resilience and emotional regulation to combat bullying and manage stressful living conditions. I wish somebody had told me to have a solid MVP (minimal viable product) before spending a lot of time and personal savings on an idea that was never going to launch. I was stubborn, and I couldn't give up on my dream. I believed that if I persisted, I would eventually get traction. But timing is everything, and I was too early in the game. You can't sell something nobody wants to buy. Prevent tunnel vision by staying focused on the longer-term and the bigger picture.

7. Embrace diversity. How can we make our company and executive team a leader in diversity and inclusion?

Recently, I saw a social media post that said, "I get tired of Under 40 lists. Show me someone who got their PhD at 60 after losing everything. Give me the 70-year-old debut novelist who writes from a lifetime of love and grief. Give me calloused hands and tender hearts."[15]

Only hiring people that think like you, look like you, always say yes, laugh at your jokes, and never challenge you is boring and will not help you or your business grow. Companies need disruptors, breakthrough agents, and novel thinkers who come in many colors, ages, genders, and religions.

8. Share the limelight. How can I let people do their jobs and be more open to others' opinions?

If you're feeling defensive about any of these points, take a breath. Getting caught up in the need for control and being a boss can be a heady trip. You can get drunk on the attention and status when you are the one everybody looks to for all the answers. It's a common phenomenon—76 percent of workers have been exposed to a toxic boss[16]. The top four types of toxic boss are:

1. The Power-Hungry Boss only looks out for themselves.

2. The Micromanager Boss doesn't trust others to do their jobs.

3. The Absentee Boss doesn't provide direction or guidance.

4. The Boss Who Sucks at His Job doesn't inspire confidence.

Learn how to be humble, delegate, and share the limelight. You'll be glad you did because I guarantee you, being on top doesn't last forever. One day your phone may stop ringing.

---

15 Bram Stoker Award-winning editor Doug Murano on Twitter.
16 Gene Marks, *Monster Poll: 76 Percent of Job Seekers Say their Boss is "Toxic"*, Inc., 2018. https://www.inc.com/gene-marks/monster-poll-76-percent-of-job-seekers-say-their-boss-is-toxic.html.

Chapter 9
COURAGE

"If you are irritated by every rub, how will your mirror be polished?"
—Rumi[17]

Suppose you are in a never-ending cycle of reactivity to whatever comes up in your business. You are stuck in a trap of responding to what's urgent versus what's important. You also feel constantly overwhelmed and stressed instead of working in a calm and planned way.

The adrenaline rush of saving something from disaster makes us feel productive. Putting out fires every day can be exhilarating, and knowing that we remain relevant strokes our ego. But without planned execution or the creation and enforcement of systems, we won't experience stability.

Before that can happen, you have to be able to give your key people autonomy to make decisions so they will feel a sense of ownership. Explain the value behind a project (the vision) and why the project makes sense (the drivers). By taking these steps, you will ensure you are in alignment, and it will empower your team members to see the impact of their work. This will ignite motivation, give them a sense of

---

17 https://en.wikipedia.org/wiki/Rumi.

ownership over tasks, and generate excitement around milestones. This is what is called getting their buy-in.

FAIL: First Attempt at Learning

To fail is the first attempt at learning something. Sometimes, the biggest bottleneck in the business is the owner. You grow a business by doing more to get more. You scale a company by doing less to get more. Scaling a business is not about less work but different work. It's work smarter, not harder.

One of the toughest things I had to learn was the courage to trust others and let go of trying to control every situation. When working with my entrepreneur clients, we talk. about the fine line between making all the decisions and knowing when to ask for help or take advice from others. It's often something they struggle with, and it can make or break the success of the company. It is what makes the difference between being a small business owner and a CEO.

A CEO asks questions instead of giving answers. They let silence do the heavy lifting and bring out the best in others, instead of placing judgment. They know how to inspire and motivate others to act and, thus, control less and influence more. And they understand the value of sharing the limelight with their team.

Another lesson I learned the hard way was that I was prone to making snap judgments, and they didn't always pan out. Malcolm Gladwell[18]'s bestselling book Blink: The Power of Thinking Without Thinking is about how our choices are formed by what seem to be instant, blink-of-the-eye decisions. The book explores the concept of "thin slicing," which refers to the ability of the human brain to make

---

18 Malcom Gladwell, *Blink: The Power of Thinking Without Thinking,* Back Bay Books, 2007.

quick and highly accurate judgments—often more accurate than decisions made after careful analysis.

The book explores examples of thin slicing in action, including how certain experts can instantaneously assess the value of works of art, how we swiftly gauge the trustworthiness of others, and how military officers make decisions in the heat of battle. These snap decisions can be based on our unconscious attitudes and prejudices, which play a huge role in our judgments. When our unconscious makes decisions for us before the conscious mind has a chance to catch up and decipher the information, it can be beneficial. But we can also be fooled when we aren't aware of our personal biases.

Consider this. Early Monday morning, you head to your office thinking about the overwhelming workload you're facing. You've been under a lot of pressure lately. You sit down at your desk and open your email. Your heart sinks when you realize you got a nasty message from one of your customers. You feel like a failure. But those emotions soon turn to irritation and anger, and you fire off an email to your assistant with the nagging feeling that the rest of the day is shot. You can't get over the feeling of being personally attacked.

Then you are interrupted by a phone call from an old friend who's in town on a short layover and you decide to meet for lunch. You head out thinking about your friend and how you haven't seen him in a long time. Over your meal, you lighten up and laugh about old times. You're amazed at his transformation and success in life. He shares story after story that leaves you feeling uplifted.

Back at your office, you feel energized and ready to tackle the day. Then you remember you need to respond to your customer. You reread the email and pause. It no longer seems to have that anger-inducing tone. You read it again and now have a completely different perspective about how to respond.

The only thing that has changed is your mood. It may sound obvious, but it can be hard to remember in the heat of the moment that our mood and emotions affect our actions and reactions.

We develop blind spots when we are unaware of our unconscious beliefs and triggers and how they affect our judgments, perceptions, and screening of external stimulate, or how we view the world around us in general. It's hard to come to grips with our blind spots. We don't know what we don't know. Blind spots can become evident when you've made a mistake, or you've ignored a certain behavior that finally produces a negative outcome. In my case, one day, someone tacked a cartoon to the lunchroom bulletin board of a famous optical illusion where from one angle, you see a beautiful young woman and from another angle, you see an old hag. I was the last to realize that it was supposed to be a depiction of me.

Blind spots rear their ugly head when you least expect them. According to Robert Bruce Shaw, author of *Leadership Blind Spots*[19], strong feelings such as overconfidence (arrogance), being ultra-positive, and being power hungry put us at risk of developing blind spots. They are difficult to identify and can affect your decision-making and problem-solving abilities. For example, a leader with a blind spot regarding diversity and inclusion may not be aware of the impact of their decisions on marginalized groups, or managers with a blind spot about communication may not realize that their message is unclear or confusing to their team.

Identifying and addressing blind spots is an important part of personal and professional development because it can help you become more self-aware and better equipped to make informed decisions and solve problems effectively.

---

19 Robert Bruce Shaw, *Leadership Blindspots: How Successful Leaders Identify and Overcome the Weaknesses That Matter*, Jossey-Bass, 2014.

Here are a few strategies you can use to identify yours.

- Seek feedback from employees, colleagues, and customers. This process can identify areas where you may be unaware of your own biases or limitations.
- Reflect on your decision-making process and how you come to conclusions. This will point to beliefs and assumptions you may not be aware of.
- Engage in personality or leadership assessments. These tools can provide you with insights into your strengths and areas for improvement.
- Work with a coach who will provide you with objective feedback and help you develop self-awareness and ways to better understand and improve your limitations so you can be more adaptable and flexible.

It's humbling to recognize your blind spots, but it is essential work. It takes self-awareness and an openness to accept feedback, whether you were seeking it or not. By embracing your mistakes or missteps, instead of ignoring them, you will be better prepared for the challenges you will face.

EXERCISE: THE MIRROR

It has been said that what we see in others is a reflection of ourselves. Or, as philosopher Jiddu Krishnamurti said, "Relationship is a mirror in which you can see yourself, not as you would wish to be, but as you are."[20] Whether we are talking about relationships with ourselves, others, colleagues, or family, they provide an opportunity for self-revelation. Understanding your relationship with yourself first will help you understand your relationship with others.

The Johari Window is an exercise developed by psychologists Joseph Luft and Harry Ingham to contextualize our relationships with ourselves and others, and see how personalities differ. It can identify strengths and areas for improvement and build more effective relationships by uncovering unconscious biases. It is based on the idea that there are four areas of self-awareness: open, blind, hidden, and unknown. The Johari Window[21] is depicted as a grid, with each of the four areas represented by a quadrant.

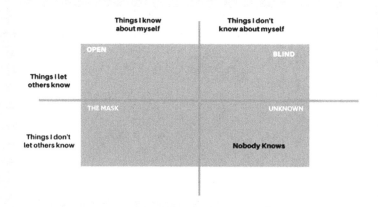

Diagram 9.1: Understanding your relationship with yourself helps you understand your relationship with other

---

20 Jiddu Krishnamurti, *Think on These Things*, HarperOne, 1989, https://www.jkrishnamurti.org/content/chapter-15.

21 Adapted from the Johari Window, created by Joseph Luft and Harrington Ingham in 1955.

To begin, select five adjectives (include words such as calm, relaxed, tense, self-assertive) that you believe describe you.

Also ask your team members or another group to pick five adjectives that describe who you are.

Compare the two lists and write them out on sticky notes. Then categorize the results in each of the four quadrants, as follows:

1. **Open self.** Adjectives selected by you and the team. This is information that is known to us and others.

2. **Hidden self.** Adjectives selected by you but not by any of your team. This is information about us that is known only to ourselves, things we hide, such as our fears, doubts, and insecurities. If most of the descriptions end up in this area, people don't know who you really are.

3. **Blind self.** Adjectives selected by your team but not you. This information about ourselves is known only to others. Adjectives in this area reveal that you don't know who you are.

4. **Unknown self.** Any adjectives not selected go into the unknown. This information is unknown to ourselves and others.

Discuss the results with the group and reflect on your findings.

Create an action plan to increase alignment with your goals.

The Johari Window can be used in a variety of ways, including:

- **Assessing team dynamics.** As a team-building exercise, everyone can gain a better understanding of their strengths and areas for improvement and learn more about their colleagues.

- **Improving communication.** Used to identify communication blind spots and to improve communication within a team or organization.

- **Facilitating personal development.** Individuals can reflect on their personal and professional development and identify areas where they can grow and improve.

  Whether you use the Johari Window as a tool for your business or personal life, it can lead to self-discovery and personal growth. Understanding the model can also help identify areas of self-awareness, improve relationships, and promote a more fulfilling life.

Chapter 10
CREATIVITY

"By failing to plan, you are preparing to fail." —*Ben Franklin*

B ack in the day, before cell phones or search engines, if you wanted information, you'd find it at a library or bookstore. I remember being disappointed that I couldn't find a book that would teach me everything I didn't know (but needed to know) about how to run a business. After all, you don't know what you don't know, and I wanted to know what I was supposed to know.

What I learned from working for my parents was the importance of a strong foundation. The fundamentals of business are the same, whether you are selling pet rocks, mowing lawns, or running a multimillion-dollar company. What entrepreneurs and experts can teach you are tips, tricks, and shortcuts to uncover creative ways to save money and make a profit. For example, my parents saved money in taxes by paying us kids to work. Instead of an allowance, we got a salary. As of this writing, you can pay up to $12,950 per child to run errands, clean your office, or do other tasks. That is a substantial way to save thousands.

I still made a ton of mistakes and was forced to learn and adapt on the spot, get comfortable with making snap decisions, and figure out how to bounce back. I felt like I was continually bouncing from one problem to the next. Instead of conducting a symphony, I was a disorganized one-man band on the brink of collapse.

One of the smartest decisions I made, in my third year of business, was to hire a summer intern from the local college. One candidate pitched me the benefits of writing a business plan. He ended up convincing me that it would help me get funding. At that point, I had been struggling for a few years, putting all my profits back into my business. I was hoping to secure a business loan to buy new equipment. I wanted to stay 100% owner and wasn't looking for partners, so a traditional bank loan was appealing.

When you create a clear vision, you open up possibilities. There are no limits to imagination. And it's well documented how visualization will give you a competitive edge. Having a business plan, road map, and blueprint that outlines your goals and objectives is key to getting you where you want to be.

A business plan is useful in attracting investors, securing funding, and staying focused and on track. Whether you are a startup or an established company, it's a valuable tool. Develop a business plan that outlines your goals, resources, and strategies. Document your target market, competition, unique selling proposition, financial projections, and long-term and short-term goals.

A road map is a high-level document that outlines a business's overall direction and strategy. It focuses on the company's key initiatives and milestones to achieve its long-term goals. A road map is excellent for communicating priorities to both stakeholders and employees.

A blueprint is a detailed plan or design that outlines the steps needed to achieve a specific goal. It can be a physical or digital document and usually includes detailed instructions, diagrams, and specifications. A blueprint is used in construction, engineering, and other industries, such as software development or marketing.

Meanwhile, a pitch deck, which is also good to have in your proverbial pocket, is a presentation of a business idea for potential investors or partners. It includes slides that provide an overview of the problem it solves, the solution, the business model, the competition, and financial potential or projections.

Benefits for all of the above include clarifying and establishing goals and benchmarks, thinking about the long and short term, and defining the strategic tactics you will use to achieve those goals. They will inspire decision-making and form a reference point from which to expand, change direction, or invest in new resources.

Whether you write your business plan on a bar napkin or present it in a more professional matter depends on your objectives. To attract investors or secure conventional bank funding, you want to prove how serious you are about your business and demonstrate your commitment to building it.

A plan, road map, blueprint, or pitch deck will help get you where you want to be while identifying potential roadblocks along the way. They enable you to assess aspects of the business you may not be paying attention to, especially if you are focused on the day-to-day grind. Communicating your vision to employees, partners, or stakeholders is vital. If people don't know where you are headed, they will likely not follow.

Hope is Not a Good Plan

One of the biggest mistakes I see business owners make is not having a plan. All of a sudden, things that were previously easy to do become difficult, such as communication and decision-making. In startup mode, you're a jack-of-all-trades. But as you grow, you need to start putting processes in place and get laser focused and specialized. Your focus should be on operational efficiency and working toward a more sustainable and manageable way of doing things.

You can quickly destroy a company if you don't align processes with overarching objectives or if you overcomplicate your systems. There needs to be a balance between effectiveness and efficiency. In Part Four of this book, we delve into the topic of efficiency in more depth. But for now, let's look at the difference between effectiveness and efficiency.

Effectiveness is the ability to accomplish specific tasks for a desired outcome. It's about doing the right things and making sure resources are being used in alignment with the goals of the company. Efficiency is the ability to accomplish a task or achieve an outcome with minimum resources. It's doing things right and making sure resources are being used in the most productive and cost-efficient way.

Striving for both effectiveness and efficiency will help you achieve optimal results. If a company is in growth mode and needs to make quick decisions and take action, efficiency rules. On the other hand, if you are trying to innovate and create new products, focus on effectiveness.

Operating efficiently means being able to use time, money, people, and equipment in a way that optimizes business processes. Companies that are efficient tend to be more profitable while delivering the same quality product or service because they use fewer resources. Regularly ask yourself, how do the tasks you are doing today tie back to the vision you have for the future?

The traditional goal of productivity is to get as much done as quickly as possible. This way of thinking is flawed because the more productive you are, the more you take on; the more you take on, the more you must produce. Your job becomes a hamster wheel of never-ending stuff to do. You get stuck in the day-to-day minutiae. This lack of planning and misalignment starts to affect every aspect of the company. But by adding efficiency to the mix, you begin increasing production by doing less. Make sense? Let me explain.

The Law of Triviality[22] was created by C. Northcote Parkinson and corroborated by behavioral research. It states that people often spend too much of their time on trivial matters and less time on bigger decisions. The reason is that major decisions require a longer time to collect information, which creates a greater window for potential errors. This is particularly true for small businesses, where resources tend to be more limited, and every decision, be it minor or significant, has a profound impact.

Organizational efficiency is in place when you are accessing your team's best talents and strengths—even if you are a solopreneur—to do the key work. It's about anticipating what needs to be done so you aren't always rushing to keep up. Managing and employing resources in a structured way helps remove yourself from the grind.

Organizational design provides a step-by-step methodology that identifies gaps or opportunities in areas such as workflow, process, and systems. Once the gaps are prioritized and realigned to fit current business goals, a plan is developed to implement and execute the new strategy.

The design process will provide a road map or blueprint that outlines how to improve results, such as increasing profitability, enhancing customer service, or empowering employees to be more engaged. The design process also covers aspects of the organization that will support endeavors such as:

---

22 C. Northcote Parkinson, *Parkinson's Law*, Blurb, 2023. https://en.wikipedia.org/wiki/Law_of_triviality.

- Reducing operating costs
- Improving cycle time (the amount of time spent on producing an item)
- Building a culture of committed team members
- Creating a strategy for scaling your business.

When you scale an organization, it's optimal to grow slowly and intentionally. The time it takes to implement new systems will distract you and make you feel you are moving away from what you do best. You lose quality communication, and even general operational knowledge seems to go out the door. But if you don't take that time, your company will become chaotic. This happens when companies don't have a good foundation or structure in place and don't anticipate or project their growth. Growing too fast forces them to either recover quickly or crash and burn.

Organizational Identity

Imagine you want to celebrate your anniversary with your loved one. You decide to book a sunset cruise in the Gulf of Mexico. As the boat pulls away from the dock, you toast and clink your glasses, excited about your night of fun and relaxation.

The captain steps forward and gets everyone's attention for an announcement.

He says, "I don't have a plan tonight, but let's hope for the best and see where we end up. The chef just told me they don't have a clue what they will serve for dinner, but I'm sure they'll figure something out. We'll just play it by ear."

How confident would you feel about the cruise now? That rapid loss of faith is what happens when business owners don't take time to work on their organizational identity. Without a clear map, you lose the potential to engage your workforce with purpose and meaning.

An organizational identity guides a company and its members' actions and decisions. A strong one can foster unity among its employees, build trust and credibility with customers and stakeholders, and provide a framework for decision-making and strategic planning. Each business has unique characteristics, values, beliefs, and purpose and is defined by history, culture, brand, reputation, and image. A company is shaped by leadership, employees, customers, stakeholders, products or services, and the environment in which it creates and operates. Getting clear on what makes your business special serves a dual purpose of differentiation and competitive advantage in a saturated marketplace.

In my experience, companies sometimes overlook the importance of developing a strong organizational identity, especially when they are focused on short-term growth or are struggling to keep up with marketplace demands. Regularly evaluate your organizational identity to remain relevant and aligned with your overall long-term objectives. Then, strengthen it through branding initiatives, marketing campaigns, employee engagement programs, and activities designed to build awareness and affinity for the business's unique value.

Aligning Organizational Identity

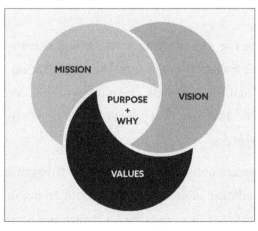

Diagram 10.1: Connecting people to how they fit with the company's purpose can be a perfor - mance driver leading to a more productive and profitable workplace

You should also plan to write a mission, vision, and values statement, which is the living expression of the company's identity. In Simon Sinek's book Start With Why[23], he says, "Knowing your WHY is not the only way to be successful, but it is the only way to maintain lasting success and have a greater blend of innovation and flexibility."

Your purpose is the WHY you exist. A mission statement explains why it exists, what it is trying to achieve, and what you do for whom. It should be specific, measurable, attainable, relevant, and time bound. It will help focus efforts and provide direction and purpose.

A vision statement represents a business's long-term goals and aspirations. It should be inspiring, clearly delineate what the organization wants to achieve, and motivate the team. It's the ultimate strategy for success.

An evolving vision is a long-term goal that changes or adapts over time. This means it's continuously updated or modified in response to changing circumstances, new information, or shifting priorities. An evolving vision allows for flexibility and innovation because it leaves room for adjustments to the original plan to ensure that it remains effective and is adaptable to changing market conditions or customer needs.

Values are the guiding principles behind culture and behavior. They reflect the beliefs necessary to the organization and provide a framework for making decisions and taking action. Values provide a sense of meaning. They can be a powerful tool for driving performance and achieving success.

It's not uncommon for companies to go through long periods of time without updating or creating clearly defined mission, vision, and values statements. Yet, it's essential to ensure you remain relevant in

23 Simon Sinek, *Start With Why: How Great Leaders Inspire Everyone to Take Action*, Portfolio, 2009.

the marketplace and remain aligned with the company's goals. When a company regularly communicates its mission, vision, and values to employees and stakeholders, and seeks feedback and input on how well they are being carried out in the organization, it can push you to the forefront of a crowded marketplace.

Next, we will talk about another way to help elevate your business, which is maintaining a dashboard and tracking data.

Dashboards and Data

In the first section of the book, we talked about the most important numbers you should be tracking. Now, let's talk about data. The nitty-gritty of the stats may make your eyes glaze over, but it's critical that you don't skip this piece of the puzzle. Tracking metrics will help identify blockages and problems that may impede your business from running efficiently. A metric can be a number, binary (yes/no, on/off), a symbol of health (red, green, yellow), or something else, but it is always a way to measure and compare. It sets expectations. If a measurement is higher or lower than expected, it's worth investigating the situation to see if a resolution is required. Make your metrics simple to understand, and they will act as the vital signs for your business's health.

A business dashboard is a visual representation of key performance indicators (KPIs) and metrics that are important for monitoring the performance of a business or organization. It can take many forms, including charts, graphs, tables, or even a combination of different visual elements, and provides an at-a-glance view of key data points. It can also be a document or a web-based platform that displays real-time or near-real-time data.

It's like your car's dashboard that displays all the relevant information you need for a safe drive; in business, it displays the operational status of things like sales, marketing, customer experience, gross profit, bank balance, and more. It lets you get an instant read on key metrics and data insights. So it's worth taking the time to determine the core metrics you want to use for your dashboard. Keep it simple, and don't get caught up tracking too many things.

Things will fail, and when they do, it's crucial to react slowly, turning the dial one notch at a time. If multiple items can change the outcome, changing those things all at once can cloud the results.

PART THREE

Put People First

Chapter 11
CULTURE

"You don't build a business. You build people, then people build the business." —Zig Ziglar[24]

When a company puts its employees first and prioritizes their well-being and development, the result is improved performance. Employees who feel valued and supported are more likely to be motivated, engaged, and committed to their work, leading to higher productivity and better results. This supportive work environment encourages creativity and innovation, leading to new ideas and approaches that can drive business growth and success.

Companies that put their people first often have a positive reputation, which can attract top talent and build a loyal customer base. This is especially critical in today's competitive job market. Companies that put their people first often have lower turnover rates, as employees are more likely to stay with an organization that values them. This can reduce the costs associated with training and onboarding new employees, and maintain continuity and stability within the organization. Putting people first is good for both the employees and the company.

---

24 Zig Ziglar, *See You at the Top: The How-to book that gives you a "Check Up" from the "Neck Up" to eliminate "Stinkin Thinkin" and AVOID "Hardening of the Attitudes"*, Pelican, 2000.

The Ship Makes the Pirate

So what is culture anyway? Ask around and you'll hear that it's about having fun, being around like-minded people, cool office designs, shared values, and screening out the wrong kinds of people, a.k.a. the bad fits.

Eric Olson, cofounder of Pedal Pub Franchise[25] told me, "It's up to the boss to create the culture. The boss hires the employees and judges whether they will fit in the culture they envision. Employees will reflect the culture they see the boss demonstrating."

Culture is often misunderstood. Some people think that if you put a ping-pong table in your warehouse and let people bring their dogs to work, that is building culture. But those are perks. Culture is connecting values to your business in a distinguishing way. Let me say that another way. It's about establishing a core set of values that drive and promote the business in perpetuity.

Why is culture important? Well, as your company grows, culture is what makes it a good place to work, preserves key values, and supports future performance. It distinguishes you from your competition, helps identify candidates that are aligned with your mission and vision, and ensures the persistence of critical operating values, such as delivering happiness or building excellence.

And it's the best way to attract and retain top talent.

Here's my short list of what it takes to build outstanding company culture:

- Clear mission and values
- Transparency
- Diversity and Inclusivity of thought, opinion, skills and competencies

---

25 https://www.franchiseopportunities.com/franchise/pedal-pub-party-bikes.

- Wins are celebrated.
- Leaders are visible and accessible.
- Team involvement in the company's success.
- Long-term employees
- Comfortable atmosphere
- Absence of office politics
- Not just colleagues, but friends
- Ongoing professional development opportunities

Create A Strengths-Based Culture

Myth: To motivate people, it's best to identify their mistakes and focus on their weaknesses to help fix them.

Reality: When you focus on people's weaknesses, their confidence suffers. This can lead to low engagement, lower productivity, and even health issues.

American psychologist Don Clifton[26] developed Clifton Strengths Analysis (formerly called Strengths Finder) to help people identify their unique abilities, based on the idea that people perform better and are more satisfied when they can use their natural strengths at work. The assessment consists of questions to identify your top five "signature themes," or core strengths, representing 34 qualities that are considered universal across cultures (e.g., strategic, achiever, adaptable, responsible, futuristic, analytical, deliberative). It can be used for teams to better understand how to leverage the strengths of their members to improve overall company performance.

Years ago, a friend of mine shared a story about why he quit working for a Fortune 500 company. He had a number of grievances,

---

26 https://en.wikipedia.org/wiki/Gallup_Test, See also StrengthsFinder 2.0, written by Tom Rath, published by Gallup Press, 2007.

but his main complaint was this—he had endured years of horribly negative performance reviews in which the message was always the same: Focus on getting rid of your weaknesses and do better next time. There's nothing worse than making you feel like you have delusions of adequacy. Well, maybe there's one thing: having to sit through a bad performance review given by incompetent managers.

Business owners may not see the value in giving performance reviews. They may procrastinate until an employee bugs them about wanting a raise. Then they trudge through the process without any direction or benefit. They point out disappointments, problem areas, and mistakes, creating a hostile work environment. Although it's common to compensate people based on performance, it can be difficult to separate someone's work from the contributions of others. But you shouldn't avoid annual performance reviews. A better approach is to find the good in people and position them so their weaknesses are minimized. This creates a much more positive experience and builds stronger trust and relationships.

Here are some other tips to avoid the pitfalls of an apathetic or negative review:

- Make it a two-way conversation.
- Share the work by having the employee fill out the documentation for your review.
- Clarify expectations, goals, and career growth.
- Focus on solutions, not problems.
- Leave out biases or inaccurate rating scales.
- Follow up.

A recent client told me she liked that I delivered negative information in a positive way. Learn to deliver feedback while empowering your employees and giving them the autonomy to make decisions so they are not constantly coming back to you with questions. To achieve peak organizational efficiency, balance your team. Determine people's strengths and put them in a position that will set them up for success. Match them to a role that will bring out their strongest characteristics. Ask your employees, "What work would you love to do?"

As you empower your team, build on their strengths, and remove bottlenecks. You will become relevant to your business in a new way. You may no longer be the heart of your company, but you will become the soul.

Having a strengths-based work culture can increase the company's ability to grow, bring out the best in your team, and allow you to retain top talent.

To recap, here are some steps you can take to champion a strengths-based work culture:

- Celebrate individual strengths.
- Encourage collaboration and teamwork.
- Foster personal and professional development.
- Emphasize positive feedback and recognition.
- Encourage open communication.

The Right Stuff with Special Sauce

There is much to be said about getting the right people in the right seat on the right bus. When Brian Scudamore, CEO of 1-800-GOT-JUNK, and author of *WTF?! How Failure Can Be Your Key to Success,*[27] was five years into his business, he realized that things were just not working out. He had eleven people working for him, and one night he realized that he would never want to sit down and have a beer with any of them. He was avoiding time in the office, he wasn't having fun anymore, and

---

27 Brian Scudamore, *WTF?! How Failure Can Be Your Key to Success,* Lioncrest, 2018.

the business wasn't delivering good customer service. He made the bold decision to fire the entire staff and start over.

It turned out to be the most monumental thing he'd ever done, and it shaped the future of the company. After that experience, he started to hire differently. "Hire for attitude; train for skill" became his mantra. He still looks for cheery people with a glass-half-full attitude. His company now has 200 locations and is worth multimillions.

One of the first systems to implement in your company is the hiring and interview process. As Brian Scudamore discovered, this is critical to your success. Hiring can't happen too soon, but it can happen too fast. If you hire too fast, you are hiring without proper consideration. Think beyond traditional roles and consider anyone or anything that can take work off your plate. There are many ways to employ contractors, virtual team members, interns, and vendors.

You need to hire, but how do you go about hiring the right person? Consider the stages of hiring to firing: attract, recruit, onboard, develop, retain, and separate. As simple as the steps are, though, nothing is that simple. In fact, it's extremely hard to know whether you've made the right hire or fire decision. It's often one of the least favorite jobs of a CEO, and something I see my clients struggle with.

Surrounding yourself with trusted advisors such as bankers, lawyers, and accountants is one thing, but hiring someone you know nothing about is another. My goal was always to hire people smarter than myself. You don't want to hire people just like you, or you won't have anyone to show you the blind spots or gaps in your understanding. You also will have to hire people for jobs that you've never done.

Here are a few things to keep in mind.

Focus on output first. Ask yourself to define the purpose of the process. In the case of interviewing, it would be to hire an outstanding employee in a given area.

Figure out how you will know if you're getting what you want. Are you seeing enough candidates? The right candidates? Once hired, will they be productive? How will you measure their progress? What are some ways you can increase their performance visibility and hold them accountable?

Find out their interests, hobbies, sports preferences, and musical talents. What do they like to do that brings them joy? Hire people with different traits than you; don't hire people you like because they will be like you. Hire people you respect. Hire people smarter than you. And don't make the mistake of hiring people based on their resumes. Skills from the past are just that, from the past. You want to hire people that have a positive, get-it-done attitude. Look for people with high energy and intelligence who are a solid cultural fit and desire to work, get ahead, and be a part of something bigger than themselves.

When you place an ad for employment, talk about your culture and why they should work for you. Put something in the ad they need to include in their response, like the word "savvy," or an intentional misspelling of a word to see if they are paying attention and reading the whole thing.

How do you build a great team? With no prior business experience and while she was homeless, Magie Cook[28] built her salsa company with a gift of $800. Over the course of a few years and 500 employees later, she sold it to Campbell's Soup for $231 million.

---

28 Magie Cook, *Mindful Success: How To Use Your Mind To Transform Your Life*, CreateSpace Independent, 2013.

Here are the attributes she looked for in the people she hired:

- Hungry for achievement
- Enthusiastic
- Energetic
- Competitive (not with others but with self)
- Interested in personal growth, has a growth mindset
- Internally motivated, connected to serving the greater good
- Solution focused
- Whatever-it-takes attitude
- Leaves crap at home; doesn't bring it to work
- Has a sense of urgency
- Able to pivot, open to change
- Open-minded about others, without regard to race, sex, religion, age.

Hiring for skills and intelligence is one thing, but they are not the only important things. People who are effective, hard-working, and team players are the ones that seem to thrive.

Creating Loyal Fans

One of my first employees was a hard worker. He taught me a lot about his job. I welcomed his training, as I instinctively knew I had to learn every job from the ground up. After all, how can you lead people when you don't know what they do? One day, I discovered a broken scientific instrument. It was an expensive piece of equipment that needed to be replaced immediately or it would halt production. Since Calvin was the only employee, and I didn't break it, it was obvious who did.

I approached Calvin and asked, "Hey, Calvin, have you seen that new hydrometer?"

"Uh, no," he said nervously.

"Well, Calvin. I know one thing: We are all human. And as humans, we make mistakes. You know you need that hydrometer to do your job. If you need something to do your job, let me know. I'm here to make sure you have everything you need to make your job easier."

After that, Calvin told every new employee, "If you break something, don't worry. Pam will make sure to replace it. She wants to make sure you have everything you need to do your job." Calvin was a loyal employee who worked for me for nearly twenty years.

That kind of loyalty is priceless. Later, I hired Tammy. During the interview, she was overtly nervous. Her resume was sparse, and she was young and inexperienced. On paper, she wasn't what I was looking for in an administrative assistant. But there was something in her that I recognized as pure potential. She had a positive, can-do attitude that hooked me into giving her a try.

Tammy was eager to learn whatever was given to her and she never complained. She had ambition and she focused on what she could do to help the company be more successful. She quickly became one of my best employees. I trained her and kept promoting her as she took on more and more responsibilities. Eventually, she was handling multiple projects and was basically my right-hand person, supporting me in everything I did.

Years later, I ran into Tammy at a restaurant. She's now a personal trainer. She introduced me to her friend as one of the best bosses she had ever had. At the time, I hadn't realized the impact of giving her the tools and resources to grow. She was the one who decided to flourish under those conditions.

Of course, sometimes you hire a dud. You may decide that you can work with the employee's bad attitude or their undermining of your authority, but there will be a cost. Managing your company and keeping everyone on the same page is hard enough without facing blatant resistance. But what do you do if that one bad apple, for all intents and purposes, seems to be doing a great job? They just don't like you and it's obvious to everyone else.

Mary was a major gatekeeper as well as a bottleneck. She fought me every chance she got. Her eye-rolling and the ways she ignored me in front of other employees when I asked for something was embarrassing. Some days, she got dressed up and took long lunches. I knew she was looking for another job and I kept thinking the problem would take care of itself, so I put up with it. Eventually, she left of her own accord.

As the leader, it's your job to be fair. If you are not careful with your words and actions, you may be sending the wrong message. I found out the hard way that being responsive and action- and solution-oriented meant I sometimes encouraged the wrong behavior. I had failed to realize that I was playing a part in office politics and drama.

To combat this, I realized I needed an airtight performance and compensation policy. Mary had been jealous of the way Tammy was being promoted. Without clear promotion guidelines in place, the bad apple felt jilted and let everyone know it. Having a well-structured performance plan in place will keep things fair and prevent bad attitudes from people who may feel undervalued.

Although there is no perfect or right way to build a performance and compensation plan, in my experience, it's best if you enlist the help of the employee as much as possible. Have them participate in filling out their own evaluation. Establish a regular time frame for reviews. Make sure you are basing promotion on merit or performance.

One thing is for sure. As your company grows, you will outgrow people. If what you hired someone for is no longer relevant and they can't keep up with changes, then you need to face the facts sooner rather than later. Don't fall into the trap of keeping people just because you like them. I never said being CEO was easy. Sometimes you have to make tough decisions and put the business first.

For the same reason, I encourage you to think long and hard before hiring family or friends. I'm not saying it can't work out, I'm saying if it doesn't work out, you have a lot to lose.

Let's talk through the right way to attract and retain top talent during the interview.

What makes your company unique. Talk about why they would want to work there and what sets you apart from the competition.

Before you start the interview, explain your process. Tell them that after you talk about your company, the position, and your expectations, you will ask some questions and then you will follow up at the end with the next steps.

Before you jump in. Ask the candidate if they agree with the process (get their buy-in) and if they have any questions.

Company culture. Make sure that your company is in alignment with your candidates by not only discussing your mission, vision, and values but sharing how these tenets are put into practice.

Know who you are looking for. Candidates will analyze the questions you ask them. Any ambiguity may make them hesitant to move forward. Don't rely on gut feelings or whether you like someone; feelings can be subjective and often turn out to be wrong.

Make sure to understand and convey these questions:

- What are the key factors required for the role?
- Which core competencies are critical?
- What other qualities and characteristics would bring the most value to the role and the organization?

- What makes someone a good fit with the team?
- In what ways will you know if they will align with the company's core values?

Plan the interview in advance. Streamline the process. Be prepared to deliver an introduction and ask the right questions. Decide in advance what questions to ask and in what order you will ask them.

Be aware of your tone and body language. The interviewer reflects the face of the company. Help candidates feel comfortable by conveying warmth, attentiveness, and interest in their professional development. Be engaged, maintain eye contact, and practice your active listening skills. Be selective of where and when the interview happens, too. Zoom or video calls have become the standard, at least for the initial interview.

Perks and benefits. Talk about what you can offer the candidate, such as benefits that may include.

- Health insurance
- Dental insurance
- Paid vacation
- A 401(k) retirement plan

Explain the special perks of the job as well. How does your company go above and beyond, and what sets it apart from the competition? What aspects of the company culture make your organization unique? Do you offer any of the following?

- Tuition reimbursement
- Wellness programs
- On-site childcare
- Volunteer days
- A casual dress code
- Snacks or free meals

- A pet-friendly office
- Hybrid work options
- 10/90 work weeks
- Annual reviews
- Quarterly or yearly bonuses.

Ask behavioral questions. In addition to your planned questions, including those specific to the candidate's resume, use strong behavioral questions as a starting point:

1. *Adaptability*. Tell me about a situation when you were under great pressure because of numerous demands competing for your time and attention. How did you resolve the situation?

2. *Customer service*. Tell me about the most difficult customer encounter you've experienced. How did you handle it?

3. *Dependability*. Tell me about a time when you had difficulty keeping a commitment. How did you handle it?

4. *Ethics*. Describe a situation in which you worked with someone you didn't like or respect. How did you cope with the relationship?

5. *Initiative*. Tell me about an opportunity that presented itself to you, but you were reluctant to take the risk. What did you do?

6. *Interpersonal skills*. Tell me about a time you had a serious conflict with a coworker. How did you handle the situation?

7. *Judgment*. Tell me about a time when you had to make a difficult decision. What process did you go through to arrive at a decision?

8. *Leadership.* Tell me about a time when you had to inspire or energize an unmotivated individual or group. How did you do it, and what was the result?

9. *Planning and organizing.* Give me a summary of the techniques you use to plan and organize your work. Describe how you applied one of these techniques in a specific situation.

10. *Teamwork.* Tell me about a time when you had to set your interests or priorities aside in the team's interest.

11. *Follow-up.* Always ask if the candidate has any additional questions. Review the next steps in the hiring process. Once you've chosen a candidate, inform the other candidates.

Chapter 12
COLLABORATION

"Let us all be the leaders we wish we had." —Simon Sinek[29]

Whether you are a solopreneur or have a big team, it's your job to see the potential in people and bring out their best. See what they are capable of becoming, even if they can't imagine it themselves. By focusing on what is good, what is right about people, their strengths, and their undiscovered positive qualities, you can show them your vision until they can see it for themselves. You stretch and challenge them to open their minds to an alternative story of what's possible.

Getting people to work together toward a common goal is the definition of collaboration. It's what being a CEO is all about. And if you are good at it, you will build a community of people with the same attitudes, interests, and goals.

As a diehard entrepreneur, I envisioned building a company where everyone worked together, had fun, and got along like one big happy family. I thought I could build a safe and friendly environment where everyone worked toward a shared vision. The vision I had was to work hard, play hard, and make money. But that vision was just a dream if I couldn't get other people to buy into what I was selling.

---

29 Simon Sinek, The Infinite Game, Portfolio, 2019. https://www.youtube.com/watch?v=xKi-lf4dVzY

Being a business owner is a struggle—an unrelenting struggle. One of the components of the struggle is dealing with people with different backgrounds, personality types, moods, emotions, and work styles. You may come to realize not everyone has the same level of drive or motivation as you. This can make it more difficult to align everyone's goals and efforts toward a common objective. The more employees you have, the more work you'll have trying to achieve this.

No Grit, No Pearl

In a 1995 interview[30] in Fortune magazine, Steve Jobs talked about the importance of teamwork. He shared a story about a rock tumbler:

> "When I was a young kid, there was a widowed man that lived up the street. He was in his eighties. He was a little scary looking. And I got to know him a little bit. I think he may have paid me to mow his lawn or something.

> "One day he said to me, 'Come on into my garage, I want to show you something.' And he pulled out this dusty old rock tumbler. It was a motor and a coffee can and a little band between them. And he said, 'Come with me.' We went out into the back and we got some rocks...some regular old ugly rocks. And we put them in the can with a little bit of liquid and a little bit of grit powder, and we closed the can up and he turned this motor on and this can was making a racket as the stones went around. And he said, come back tomorrow.

> "When I came back the next day, we opened the can. And we took out these amazingly beautiful, polished rocks. The same common stones that had gone in, through

---

30 Philip Elmer-Dewitt, *Steve Jobs: The Parable of the Stones,* Fortune magazine, November 11, 2011.

rubbing against each other, creating a little bit of friction, creating a little bit of noise, had come out these beautiful, polished rocks. That's always been, in my mind, my metaphor for a team working really hard on something they're passionate about.

"It's that through the team, through that group of incredibly talented people bumping up against each other, having arguments, having fights sometimes, making some noise, and working together they polish each other and they polish the ideas, and what comes out are these really beautiful stones."

When great forces collide to smooth out the rough edges, that's when a team can really soar. When I started my company, it would have benefitted me to better understand different personality traits and types. It took me a while to learn to recognize ways to engage and manage people effectively. Having insights into someone's go-to traits, especially when they are under pressure, can help in negotiations and influencing or motivating others. More important, it can help you be more empathic, self-aware, and understanding.

There is huge value in showing compassion to others versus being sympathetic, which is when you are glad you don't have the same problems. Empathy is something you can learn. It's not a sign of weakness; it's a sign of emotional and cognitive intelligence. Unfortunately, it also seems to be on the decline in America. One recent study[31] reported that 25% of Americans find that empathy "doesn't matter," although an overwhelming majority (73%) agree it would be better for society if people were more empathetic. Some 42% say

---

31 "Report: Is Empathy Dead in America?" Method Communications, Oct. 27, 2021. https://www.prnewswire.com/news-releases/report-is-empathy-dead-in-america-301409622.html.

empathy has declined over the past years, and of these, more than 80% are concerned about the decline." The good news is that most people are capable of developing empathy when they understand the value of tuning into the personalities of those around them.

Over the years, there have been many frameworks describing individual differences in personality and behavior. Some of the best known include the Myers-Briggs Type Indicator (MBTI), the Five Factor Model (FFM), and the Enneagram of Personality.

The Myers-Briggs assessment identifies individual differences in how people perceive the world and make decisions. It's based on four dimensions, with each having two possible preferences: extraversion versus introversion, sensing versus intuition, thinking versus feeling, and judging versus perceiving.

The Five-Factor Model identifies five broad dimensions of personality:

Openness versus being closed to experience. The former includes a willingness to try new things, to be vulnerable, and to think outside the box.

Conscientiousness versus lack of direction. This identifies whether you act in socially acceptable ways, control impulses, have goal-directed behavior, work within the rules, and plan and organize effectively.

Extroversion versus introversion. The two ends of this spectrum here reveal where someone gets their energy and how they recharge, whether it's drawn from interacting with others or replenishing with solitude.

Agreeableness versus antagonism. This refers to how people interact or get along with others, whether they are sensitive to the needs of others, whether they are affectionate.

Neuroticism versus emotional stability. This reflects being comfortable in your own skin, general temperament, and self-consciousness and/or insecurity.

The Enneagram identifies nine different personality types, each associated with a certain set of characteristics and behaviors. It's based on the idea that everyone is driven by one of the nine core fears or desires, and their personality type is shaped by how they cope with them.

As a business owner, it's a good idea to have a basic understanding of personality types, whichever model resonates for you. When you can easily recognize certain characteristics, you will be more prepared to adjust your approach and become aware of how you come across and communicate.

No personality trait is better or worse than any other; we are more than the sum of our traits. Depending on which model you look at, you can be one of five, nine, or sixteen different personality types.

There are so many ways to recognize and appreciate diversity, but for simplicity's sake, **I've reduced the main behavioral categories to four that you will recognize among your workers and colleagues:**

Extrovert or introvert. Extroverts are outgoing, sociable, and energetic, while introverts are more introspective, reserved, and independent.

Conscientious or spontaneous. Conscientious people are organized, reliable, and disciplined, while spontaneous people are more flexible, adaptable, and open to new experiences.

Logical or emotional. People who are logical tend to rely on reason and analysis to make decisions, while emotional individuals may be more influenced by their feelings and values.

Cooperative or competitive. Cooperative people value collaboration and teamwork, while competitive individuals may be more focused on achieving their own goals and outperforming others.

Bringing Out the Best in Others

One-on-one discussions between leaders and employees are powerful if done right, with acknowledgment of the different ways that everyone functions and communicates. It should be a free-form meeting outlining all the pressing issues, brilliant ideas, and chronic frustrations that do not fit neatly into an email, in status reports, or in other less personal means. The employee sets the agenda. The leader asks questions and listens 90 percent of the time and gives advice or talks only about 10 percent of the time. Some of the best questions involve empowering the employee so they feel you are supporting them and providing them with the tools they need to get the job done. In Marcia Reynolds'[32] book *Coach the Person, Not the Problem*, she says, "Coaching should be a process of inquiry, not a series of questions. The intent of inquiry is not to find solutions but to provoke critical thinking about our own thoughts."

Here are some examples of questions I've used to stimulate a more conversational approach that leads to breakthrough ideas:

Is there anything you need to help you do your job better?

What's the number one thing preventing you from doing your job effectively?

If we could improve and make your job easier, how could we do that?

What don't you like about your job or this company?

---

32 Marcia Reynolds, *Coach the Person, Not the Problem: A Guide to Using Reflective Inquiry,* Berrett-Koehler, 2020.

What's the biggest opportunity that we are missing?

What else are we missing? What are we not doing that we should be doing?

The bottom line, the most important thing, is to hash out good ideas, learn about problems before they become big, and find out if the employee is dealing with any life issues that may affect their performance.

As much as you think your business revolves around you, you are replaceable. By the same token, if the company is 100 percent dependent on you, that is not sustainable. Teaching others to support you in your role will help eliminate this problem. The best student is always the teacher.

To make sure you're taking advantage of the unique skills and qualities of your people, schedule a check-in with anyone that you haven't spoken to in a longer format in a while. Meet one-on-one with each employee to learn about their individual needs and specify optimal procedures and expectations. Use daily huddles to highlight how people are making both big and small improvements and empower employees to teach and learn from each other. Have employees share their perceived best practices as well.

Constantly swooping in to fix things may backfire as employees view this as interference. Your workers may be too timid to speak up, even when they have a great idea, thinking they couldn't possibly have a better idea than their boss. Ask your employees for solutions regularly. They are in the trenches and may know best how to improve things. Ask, "Is there anything we need to change to make the job better for you?"

Increasing Employee Engagement

Regularly checking in with your employees is also critical to stem the tide of disengagement at work. According to Gallup, in 2021, for the first time in over a decade, employee engagement declined, which made sense during the pandemic-driven chaos, but this is a challenge that you will need to actively and regularly address. Here's the kicker: Gallup also found that 75 percent of millennials are engaged at work, but this only applies to millennials working remotely. The desire for flexibility and work-life balance is a huge factor in whether employees remain on board. These days, employers face many challenging decisions, such as planning for hybrids of remote and on-site work and trying to match company goals and objectives with worker preferences.

Employee engagement is about the level of commitment, involvement, and enthusiasm that employees have towards their work, their company, and their leaders. Working to increase engagement can improve performance, increase productivity, and reduce turnover.

Here are some approaches to boosting engagement:

Provide information. Employees are more likely to be engaged when they understand the purpose and goals of the organization and how their work contributes to the whole. Clearly communicating the company's mission, vision, and values is key.

Offer opportunities for growth and development. When you provide training or mentorship opportunities and leadership development programs, you help people stay engaged and motivated.

Foster a positive work culture that values and respects employees. This includes creating a supportive and inclusive work environment and recognizing and rewarding employees for their contributions.

Encourage open communication and collaboration by allowing employees to have a voice in decision-making. This can be achieved by having regular team meetings and soliciting feedback and input to promote teamwork.

Focus on well-being and work-life balance. This can be anything from health, social, and community connectedness or, on a grander scale, working for the greater good and incorporating conscious capitalism, sustainability, and social impact into organizational goals.

Leaders determine whether their employees are fully engaged or not. Ensure real emotional engagement by focusing on the manager-employee relationship. Managers who encourage employees to demonstrate engagement externally through their actions also drive commitment. There is a need for a strong employee value proposition, balancing training, access to new skills, and long-term employment.

To show your diverse team that you value what they each bring to the table, your goals should be:

- Leadership that supports rather than dictates.
- Supporting career progression.
- Getting to know what motivates your team members.
- Being open and consistent.
- Showing gratitude.
- Amplifying accomplishments.
- Communicating well and often.
- Emphasizing positive feedback.

One of the keys to successful one-on-ones between leaders and employees is understanding and acknowledging the different personality types and communication styles of everyone involved. By allowing the employee to set the agenda and listening to them 90 percent of the time, leaders can empower their staff to feel supported while providing them the tools they need to excel. And by focusing on the manager-employee relationship and creating a strong value proposition, leaders can ensure their employees are more engaged, motivated, and committed to the mission of the company.

Chapter 13

CONFLICT

"The fairest thing we can experience is the mysterious. It is the fundamental emotion which stands at the cradle of true science. He who knows it not, and can no longer wonder, can no longer feel amazement, is as good as dead. We all had this priceless talent when we were young. But as time goes by many of us lose it. The true scientist never loses the faculty of amazement. It is the essence of his being."
—Hans Selye, Founder of Stress Theory[33]

People start a business with the dream of being their own boss, finding financial independence, and controlling their future. They might also want to positively impact their community or world. Owning a business allows you to use your creativity to nourish something new and innovative, enable you to pursue your goals, and focus on your passion for a cause or desire to solve a problem. But—and it's a big but— owning a business is hard. The struggle is real. Your success will depend on what you decide to do with the challenges you face.

Managing Stress

At some point, you will feel like you are on a constant whitewater rafting trip—always behind, overwhelmed, and exhausted. Too many times, I've seen that state become the norm. But it is something you need to get under control, or you will forever find yourself treading water. According to Forrest Gump, if you have to cry, do it by yourself

---

33 Lily Rothman, *Meet the Doctor Who Changed Our Understanding of Stress*, Time, March 10, 2016. https://time.com/4243311/hans-selye-stress/.

and be quick about it. It's just when things are picking up that something else will fall apart.

In Zen Buddhism, the phrase "the obstacle is the path" speaks to the idea that challenges can be growth opportunities to learn and develop new skills and perspectives. We find those aha moments when we embrace obstacles rather than avoid them. We must shift our mindset from resistance and avoidance to acceptance and openness to change, which happens by getting in alignment with our purpose. Whenever I'm trying to wrap my mind around a situation that feels impossible, I like to return to the following parable[34]:

> In medieval China, there once lived an old farmer who had a weak, ailing horse to plow his field. One day, the sickly horse ran away to the hills.
>
> The farmer's neighbors offered their sympathy, "Such rotten luck!" they exclaimed.
>
> "Good luck? Bad luck? Who knows?" said the farmer.
>
> A week later, the old horse returned, bringing with it a herd of wild horses from the hills. This time, the neighbors swarmed around the farmer and congratulated him on his good luck. His reply, however, was the same: "Good luck? Bad luck? Who knows?"
>
> Sometime later, while trying to tame one of the wild horses, the farmer's only son fell off its back and broke his leg. Everyone thought this was bad luck.
>
> "Bad luck? Good luck? I don't know," said the farmer.
>
> A few weeks later, the king's army marched into the village and enlisted every able-bodied young man. The farmer's son with the broken leg was thought to be of no use to them, so he wasn't enlisted.

---

34 https://en.wikipedia.org/wiki/The_old_man_lost_his_horse.

Once again, the farmer said, "Good luck or bad luck? Who can tell?"

Although there is discord in the world, there is also an underlying harmony. We don't really know why things happen the way they do, and what the resulting outcome will be. I've found this especially useful to remember when I'm feeling extra stressed, or when I see one of my employees struggling.

I also try to keep in mind that not all stress is created equal. For example, "eustress" is a type of stress that is positive and motivating. It's like applying some healthy pressure to get inspired. It can help individuals perform at their best and achieve their goals. Eustress is often associated with excitement and challenge, and it can make people feel energized. In the workplace, it can be a useful tool for helping employees stay focused and motivated when working on a project they are passionate about or when they are given a new challenge they are excited to tackle. Eustress can also allow employees to stay on track when working toward a goal or deadline.

Of course, like all stress, eustress can turn negative if it becomes overwhelming or if it is not managed effectively. Today's stressors are usually mental and result in habitual thought and negative self-talk, such as should, shouldn't, can't, must, have to, always, never, everyone. Encourage your employees to engage in positive self-talk and frame their self-talk in questions, such as "What's the lesson here?" "What am I missing?" "How can I learn from this? "Is there something else to this?" Individuals and organizations need to find a balance between healthy levels of stress and relaxation to maintain overall well-being and productivity.

Manage stress among your people (and yourself) for a more constructive workplace for everyone. The most useful approach will vary depending on the individual's needs and preferences, but **some common strategies to manage stress include:**

Physical activity. Regular physical activity, which can reduce stress and improve overall physical and mental health.

Prioritizing tasks. Work on the tough things first or last, whichever you find most effective.

Time management. Find a system that allows you to prioritize tasks, reduce workload, and control your schedule.

Delegation. Delegating can reduce your burden and allow you to focus on your most important responsibilities.

Present-moment practices. Practices such as mindfulness and meditation can help you stay in the moment and reduce stress.

Seeking support. Reach out to friends, family, or a professional such as a therapist or coach to help manage stress.

It's worth taking the time to find strategies that work for you and to be proactive in seeking support when needed. You can be a better leader, not to mention a better spouse, parent, citizen, and more, when you are regulated and able to walk in the world as your best self.

Managing Emotions

You may have heard of "being in a flow," which was famously coined by positive psychologist Mihaly Csikszentmihalyi. He describes flow as a state in which people are so involved in an activity that nothing else seems to matter. Flow is also known as being "in the zone," where you lose track of time while doing something.

Flow is conducive to peak performance and optimal functioning, allowing a person to engage in an activity while being fully present. It also has many psychological and physical benefits, including increased happiness, creativity, and improved mental and physical well-being.

Being in a flow is undoubtedly awesome, but what about those stages in between when you are overwhelmed, stressed, and disengaged? It's hard to be in a flow when you run a business, wear many hats, and must do stuff that doesn't feel natural, or when day-to-day stressors emerge, as they inevitably do.

On your worst days, you might feel anything but the happiness of flow. An emotional hijack, also known as an amygdala hijack, refers to a sudden, intense emotional response to a stimulus that takes over an individual's thinking and behavior. It is characterized by a strong emotional reaction that is out of proportion to the situation and can result in impulsive or irrational behavior, often a fight-or-flight response to stress.

Emotional hijacks are believed to be caused by the amygdala, a small almond-shaped area in the brain responsible for processing emotions and triggering the body's fight-or-flight response. When the amygdala perceives a threat or danger, it signals the rest of the body to prepare for immediate action. This can lead to a rapid and intense emotional reaction, such as anger or fear.

Emotional hijacks can be triggered by various stimuli, including personal attacks, criticism, or perceived threats. They can also be caused by physiological factors, such as fatigue or stress.

We should all be aware of our emotional triggers and try to manage our emotions to avoid emotional hijacks. This can involve practicing mindfulness and self-regulation techniques, such as deep breathing or counting to ten before reacting.

It is important to manage emotions in the workplace for several reasons:

Improved productivity. When employees can manage their emotions effectively, they can better focus on their work and be more productive.

Enhanced teamwork. Managing emotions can create a positive and supportive work environment, fostering teamwork and collaboration.

Improved communication. When people can manage their emotions, they can better communicate with their colleagues and resolve conflicts positively.

Enhanced decision-making. Managing emotions can help people make better decisions because they are less likely to be swayed by negative emotions such as anger or fear.

Increased job satisfaction. When employees can manage their emotions, they may be more satisfied and experience greater well-being.

Enhanced leadership. Leaders who can effectively manage their emotions are often seen as more effective and are better able to inspire and motivate their team.

Managing emotions in the workplace can lead to a more positive and productive work environment for everyone involved. **There are several strategies that a business owner can use to manage their own emotions and the emotions of their staff:**

Set an example. Manage your own emotions effectively and model positive emotional behavior for your staff to follow.

Communicate openly. Encourage open and honest communication within your team. This will foster a positive and supportive work environment and will allow team members to express their emotions and concerns in a safe space.

Provide training. Consider offering your staff training or resources on emotional intelligence and emotional management. This can help them better understand and manage their own emotions and the emotions of others.

Encourage self-care. Encourage your team to prioritize self-care and provide resources or support to help them manage their emotions and well-being.

Address conflicts. If conflicts or negative emotions arise within your team, address them promptly and effectively. Use conflict resolution strategies such as active listening, empathy, and problem-solving to resolve issues for a positive outcome.

Seek support. If you or your team are struggling with negative emotions, consider seeking support from a professional such as a therapist or counselor.

Overall, managing emotions in the workplace requires effective communication, training, and support. If you put in the effort to lead by example, that alone will go far in creating a positive and productive work environment.

Our emotions are closely linked to our physical and mental states.

Strategies that have helped me make beneficial shifts include:

Physical activity. Engaging in physical activity naturally makes an impact on your physical state and has a positive effect on your emotions.

Breathing. Taking slow, deep breaths can calm the mind and body, which then shifts your emotional state. There are two methods worth mentioning: deep breathing and belly breathing. Both work towards stress management and relaxation and may be used as part of a broader practice of mindfulness or meditation.

Deep breathing is a general term that refers to taking slow, deep breaths to promote relaxation and manage stress. There are various techniques.

Belly breathing, also known as diaphragmatic breathing or abdominal breathing, is a type of deep breathing that involves focusing on the movement of the diaphragm, a muscle located at the base of the lungs. When you belly breathe, you inhale deeply through your nose and exhale through your mouth, allowing the diaphragm to expand and contract fully. This type of breathing is recommended for stress management, relaxation, and improving respiratory function.

Positive affirmations. Repeating affirmations to yourself, such as "I can accomplish anything I put my mind to," can reframe negative thoughts and transform your emotional state.

Focusing on good memories. Thinking about good memories or experiences can shift your emotional state to a more positive place.

Changing your surroundings. Surrounding yourself with positive influences and moving into a happier environment can shape your emotions.

Social psychologist and bestselling author Amy Cuddy[35] has researched the connections between how we move—or "power poses"— and our emotions, confidence, and hormones. In short, a power pose is a life hack to make you feel confident and energized. In her research, Cuddy has found that people who adopt expansive, open, and confident postures experience increased testosterone (a hormone associated with confidence) and decreased cortisol (the stress hormone). She also found that people who adopt these power poses tend to perform better in stressful situations.

Power poses include standing with hands on hips, standing with feet wide apart and hands on hips, and sitting with hands behind the head and arms akimbo. These postures are believed to promote

35 Amy Cuddy, *Presence: Bringing your Boldest Self to Your Biggest Challenges*, Little, Brown Spark; First Edition, 2015.

confidence, power, and control. Try a power pose to boost your self-esteem and reduce stress in the workplace, while public speaking, and in your personal relationships. They may also be used as part of a broader practice of mindfulness or self-care.

Managing Chaos

Many factors can contribute to chaos in the workplace, including:

Lack of clear communication. When there isn't clear communication between team members or between management and employees, it can lead to confusion and misunderstandings.

Poor organization. A disorganized workplace leads to employees struggling to find what they need or stay on top of their tasks.

High-stress levels. A high-stress work environment means overwhelmed employees who are unable to manage their workload or responsibilities effectively.

Lack of clear goals and expectations. When objectives or expectations are unclear, it can be difficult for team members to know what they are working towards. It can lead to chaos if they don't understand the priority of their tasks.

Inadequate resources. A lack of resources, such as tools, equipment, or support, can make it difficult for employees to complete their work effectively.

Poor leadership. Ineffective or unpredictable leadership may mean that team members don't know what is expected of them or how to work together effectively.

Big changes. Major shifts in processes or the workforce can lead to disorder as people adjust to new roles and responsibilities. If growing your business is your goal, how do you prevent accelerating too fast, which could lead to a chaos?

Fundamental signs that will set you spinning into the danger zone and ways to prevent it:

Losing track of money. Nothing will get you in trouble faster than losing track of your finances and budget. I've devoted half of this book to making financials your superpower for this reason. Watch your numbers regularly and take action quickly if anything is amiss.

Cash isn't flowing. Don't lose track of what it means to be profitable. Stay on top of your accounts receivable, so you don't feel your gut sinking when you realize that one of your largest clients has just defaulted on a payment. This is a no-brainer, but I'm going to say it anyway: Make sure you bring in more money than you are spending.

Shooting for the moon. Projections are great, and being overly optimistic is a nice trait, but how realistic are your sales estimates? Tracking how much revenue you have coming in is the first step, but make sure you also weigh all the what-ifs and have a Plan B in case you didn't make a solid business decision based on your analysis of the situation.

When the evil twin shows up. I used to joke, just hire them if they are breathing. One time, I hired a guy that checked all the boxes, but when he showed up to work the next day, I could have sworn it was his evil twin.

All jokes aside, when you're in growth mode, you may get desperate and hire people without taking the time to ensure they are the right fit. Of course, you may need to make compromises along the way—just be clear about what you will give up for the skills you need.

Assess your gaps. The faster you grow, the more processes you will need to have in place. You won't be behind the eight ball if you wait until everything is flowing nicely before you document processes. Assess how organized your company is. Does everyone know their role and responsibilities? Do you have clearly defined core principles that everyone is aware of? If not, take time to put those in digital or written format.

Decision time. There's nothing more degrading than micromanagement, other than no management at all. Don't lose track of the big picture, but don't get stuck in the minutiae. A good manager knows that a bad decision is better than no decision at all. Take risks but know when to pivot or do a pirouette. Whatever you call it, know when you're ready to bounce back from mistakes, learn from them, own them, and move on.

Customer service fails. If you google "consumers would rather clean a toilet than call customer service," you get millions of results. Without proper planning, nothing goes out the window faster than quality service. Maintaining good customer service as you grow is a must. I built my company slower than some competitors because I was interested in providing prompt, quality service, which was our tagline. That focus was the secret to our success and longevity.

Beam me up, Scotty. Not having the right technology in place, or having too much technology, is asking for trouble. I've known companies that have been in each situation, and both are risky. Although every company has different requirements, know what solutions are best for you. Don't cause more chaos by changing software at the last minute and make everyone scramble to learn a new system while under time pressure and stressed out, and don't have too many platforms that make things even less efficient and confusing.

Healthy Conflict

It's common for people to avoid conflict at all costs, whether that's because we find it uncomfortable or stressful, or because we value harmony and try to maintain positive relationships with others. Some people may also avoid conflict because they feel that it is not worth the effort or that it will not lead to a productive resolution. As my mother used to say, pick your battles.

However, avoiding conflict can have negative consequences. If some friction is not addressed and resolved, it can lead to resentment, misunderstandings, and strained relationships. In some cases, avoiding conflict may also mean not standing up for what you believe in or not addressing issues that need to be addressed. It is important to find a balance and to be able to effectively handle conflict in a healthy and productive manner when it arises.

When I talk about healthy conflict in the workplace, I'm referring to the idea that it is normal and even beneficial for individuals to disagree. When handled effectively, these differences can lead to creative problem-solving, better decision-making, and stronger relationships.

Here is an example of healthy conflict in the workplace:

Two colleagues are working on a project together and have different ideas about how to approach it. One believes that the best approach is to complete all the tasks in sequential order, while the other thinks it would be more efficient to work on tasks in parallel. They discuss their differing viewpoints and listen to each other's perspectives. They consider the pros and cons of each approach. They ultimately decide to try working on tasks in parallel, with the understanding that they can always adjust their approach if needed.

These coworkers engaged in healthy conflict by focusing on the issue at hand, seeking to understand each other's viewpoints, and using respectful communication. They were also open to the possibility of changing their own perspectives. In the process, they found a resolution that worked for both of them.

Some characteristics of healthy conflict in the workplace include:

- Focusing on the issue at hand, rather than personal attacks
- Seeking to understand other viewpoints and perspectives
- Being open to the possibility of changing one's own viewpoint
- Using respectful and professional communication
- Seeking resolution and finding a way forward that works for everyone

Conflict in the workplace can become unhealthy if it is not managed effectively. Unhealthy conflict can lead to negative emotions, damaged relationships, and decreased productivity. Individuals and organizations must have strategies in place for addressing and resolving disputes in a healthy way.

As spiritual teacher Eckhart Tolle[37] has said: The ego believes that through negativity it can manipulate reality and get away with it....Whenever you are unhappy, there is the unconscious belief that the unhappiness "buys" you what you want. If "you"—the mind—did not believe that unhappiness works, why would you create it? The fact is, of course, that negativity does not work. Instead of attracting a desirable condition, it stops it from arising....Its only useful function is that it strengthens the ego, and that is why the ego loves it.

The solution is to become more present and more aware of what thoughts are circulating in your mind. Choose to make your mind an interesting, adventurous place. Chose to focus on healthy conflict and get rid of the drama, mama.

---

37 Eckhart Tolle, *The Power of Now: A Guide to Spiritual Enlightenment*, New World Library, 1ˢᵗ Edition, 1999.

EXERCISE: PRIME YOUR BRAIN FOR PEAK PERFORMANCE

Neuroscientists have discovered a way to keep your mind sharp, energize your body, and release stress and tension. It only takes a few minutes, and you can do it anywhere. All you have to do is a few simple exercises to activate opposite sides of the brain. The corpus callosum, a large bundle of nerve fibers that connects the left and right hemispheres of the brain, is responsible for transmitting information and communication between the two hemispheres.

There are several potential benefits to activating the corpus callosum:

- Improved cognitive function
- Enhanced creativity
- Improved memory. This includes memory consolidation, which is the process by which temporary memory is transferred into a more stable and long-lasting form
- Enhanced emotional regulation

Here are some simple exercises to sync the hemispheres of your brain:

- Pat your head and rub your tummy.
- Write using your non-dominant hand.
- Cross your arms as you normally would, then try to cross them the opposite way.
- Read the names of colors that are written in different colors than their names. This is otherwise known as the Stroop test, named after psychologist John RidleyStroop.[36]
- Cross-crawl, which refers to movements where the opposite sides of your body work together, such as crawling, walking, and swimming.
- Juggle.

---

36 https://thedecisionlab.com/thinkers/psychology/john-stroop.

By using these strategies and the others we've discussed, you can learn to shift your emotions in a more positive direction, enhance your whole-brain thinking, and be the boss and leader that you want to be.

Although activating the corpus callosum has potential benefits, note that more research is needed to fully understand its effects.

EXERCISE: HEALTHY CONFLICT

Some ground rules of healthy conflict:

- No interruptions (turn off phones)
- Exercise will take 45 minutes, with 15 minutes left for wrap-up.
- Have paper/pen ready for notes.
- Review the purpose, agenda, solutions, and outcome.

   Here's an example of what this might look like:

   Purpose. The purpose of the meeting today is to lay the foundation for a more productive and collaborative working relationship.

   Agenda. The agenda is to uncover gaps in roles and responsibilities and blind spots in communication, processes, and leadership.

   Solutions. We will focus on identifying issues and brainstorming solutions.

   Outcome. The outcome will be to clear the air and reach an agreement that is in alignment with the company's goals, vision, and values.

Review of the Go-Round Process

The mediator opens by directing this question to the first person: "Tell us about the situation you are dealing with from your point of view."

The first person begins the go-round[8]. Their job is to speak about anything on their mind, whether it's an issue or situation they are dealing with, concerns, feelings, needs, and wants. If it's easier, they can talk directly to the mediator. The second person's job is to listen. Save any responses, comments, or questions for later. If you need to, write down anything you want to remember to say. That way, each person will get their full turn.

As the first person speaks about their experience, the second person tries to notice anything they say that's new to them. You may hear things that surprise you or that you strongly disagree with, and they may not square up with your own point of view or perspective. That's okay. We will discuss it later, after each person has had their turn to talk. Then we will switch to the other person. (We will flip a coin to see who goes first.)

Each person will take as much time as needed.

While the other person is speaking, resist the impulse to judge or make assumptions. Be open and listen in a way that shows that you hear the other person and that you are open to what they are saying.

There will be no solving or discussion until after each person has a go-round, a chance to talk, without interruptions or challenges.

After each person has presented their side, we will begin an open discussion.

Open Discussion

Think of the open discussion this way: it's like cleaning out your closet. It looks like a huge task and mess, and you wonder how you will ever get it organized, but you have to start by dumping all the stuff out and seeing what's there.

---

38 Freely adapted from *The Mediator's Handbook* by Jennifer E. Beer and Caroline C. Packard, with Eileen Stief, New Society, 2012.

This part is where we embrace healthy conflict and uncover and discuss miscommunications or unintended slights that have been brewing under the surface. We will sort through the jumble and clear up gaps or misinformation to gradually build a clearer picture of the situation.

Ideally, we will shift from a problem mindset to a solution mindset, which will take us to the next part, the agreement. The last fifteen minutes will be focused on walking away with clear action items. Ready?

Reaching an Agreement

We will answer the following questions, which is part of planning for the future:

- What steps do we need to take?
- What steps are the most crucial?
- How to communicate in the future should problems arise again?

Examples of solutions:

- Clearly define roles and responsibilities.
- Align vision and values.
- Develop procedures for routine tasks.
- Hold regular meetings.
- Track and measure goals and expectations

Once an agreement is acceptable for both parties, create a document that outlines the details, lists a review-by date, and have both parties sign.

Wrap-Up

Wrap-up questions to cover:

- What are examples of the behavior and what was the impact?
- What other topics do we need to talk about?
- Could you summarize what's most important to you?

Conflict is an inevitable part of life, and it can be handled in a productive way. Healthy conflict in the workplace can lead to better decision-making, creative problem-solving, and enhanced relationships. Avoiding conflict may seem the path of least resistance, but it can lead to negative outcomes in the long run when relationships become strained due to unspoken resentment or unresolved issues. Effective communication, active listening, and a willingness to consider different perspectives are the key components to handling conflict in a healthy way.

PART FOUR

How To Be Effectively Efficient

Chapter 14
COMMUNICATION

"I was a little excited but mostly blorft. 'Blorft' is an adjective I just made up that means 'completely overwhelmed but proceeding as if everything is fine and reacting to the stress with the torpor of a possum.' I have been blorft every day for the past seven years." — Tina Fey, Bossypants[39]

Theodore Roosevelt famously said, "Speak softly and carry a big stick." Big stick policy may have worked in 1901, but that was then and this is now. In his book *The Hard Things About Hard Things*, Ben Horowitz[40] notes, "Sometimes an organization doesn't need a solution; it just needs clarity."

Having clarity involves effective communication, not just the words you speak. Albert Mehrabian[41], a body language researcher, has found that the message or the emotional impact of communication is 55 percent nonverbal—think of hand gestures, posture, and body language. The vocal aspects of speech, such as pitch, tone, and pace, make up 38 percent, and the words we use comprise only 7 percent of communication. With the shifting workplace landscape, we are changing the way we communicate. In digital meetings, without being able to

---

39 Tina Fey, *Bossypants*, Back Bay Books, 2012.
40 Ben Horowitz, *The Hard Thing About Hard Things: Building a Business When There Are No Easy Answers*, Harper Business, 2014.
41 Albert Mehrabian, *Silent Messages: Implicit Communication of Emotions and Attitudes*, Wadsworth, 1908. https://www.bl.uk/people/albert-mehrabian.

pick up on body language or social cues, we may be misinterpreting things that previously would have been resolved quickly in the office.

To be an effective leader, you must be able to express yourself clearly. You must have an opinion about everything. Whether it's presentations, comments, or forecasts, people should know what you think. If you like someone's performance, say so. If you don't like someone's comment in a meeting, say so. But just because you have an opinion doesn't always mean you are right. The other person may know more about their job and situation than you do. Be open to listening to what they say. Encourage people to challenge their judgment. Allow them time to argue their point. You want to be open enough to find out when you are wrong and making bad decisions. You want to set high standards and develop high-quality thinking in your team.

The Power of Words

A CEOs most important responsibility is designing and implementing the company's communication architecture, meaning the flow of information between the company, the individuals in the company, and the outside world. When you have transparent processes, you have greater communication. Nothing hurts a business more than a failure to have clear internal and external communication channels and directives. Make sure to dictate what tools are used with what system. Linear communication can go awry when using Slack, text, and email.

Prepare for growth by incorporating communication and decision-making processes:

- What needs to be communicated?
- List the knowledge and who needs to have it.
- What needs to be decided?
- Consider the types of decisions and how frequently they

need to be resolved.

- Prioritize the most important decision paths.
- Who will run or drive the work, who will contribute to the work, who will approve the work, and who needs to be informed of the work?
- When will you wrap up the work?
- What are the next steps including due dates, timelines, and expectations?

Although nonverbal communication is huge, words are still powerful, of course. When plants are exposed to kind words, they grow healthier and grow more than plants that are yelled at. If words can impact plants so deeply, imagine what they can do to humans. Words and intentions (energy and vibrations) may even alter the molecular structure of water. Since we are made mostly of water, do words, thoughts, and intentions have the ability to either strengthen or weaken us?

Words can lift you up, and make you feel better, but they can also hurt. The way your brain responds to words can affect the way you experience the world. In their book, Words Can Change Your Brain, neuroscientist Dr. Andrew Newberg and communications expert Mark Robert Waldman say, "A single word has the power to influence the expression of genes that regulate physical and emotional stress."[42] Our considered thoughts can literally change our reality. By holding onto positive thoughts about ourselves, we can also train our brains to see the good in others. Even the Bible notes, "Be careful what you think because your thoughts run your life." (Proverbs 4:23).

The "unconscious mind" refers to the mental processes that occur outside of our conscious awareness. It is not capable of understanding

---

42 Andrew Newberg and Mark Robert Waldman, *Words Can Change Your Brain: 12 Conversation Strategies to Build Trust, Resolve Conflict, and Increase Intimacy*, Avery, 2012.

language or abstract concepts in the same way that our conscious mind is, and it is believed to play a role in memory, learning, and the regulation of emotions and behaviors.

Start by paying attention to how you speak to yourself and what you say in conversation. Do certain words have different physical and emotional impacts? Here's what I mean. Don't think of a pink flamingo. Do not see that flamingo putting its foot down. Don't think about biting into a lemon. Don't feel how that lemon makes you pucker up. Well, it can't be done! In order for you not to think of or imagine something, you have to think or imagine it first. That's because your unconscious mind cannot compute something that is not.

The brain doesn't register don't or not (negative adverbs or contractions). Words are powerful, especially in the way the brain hears them. If you say, "I don't feel well," it doesn't have the same squirmy effect in your stomach as the words "I feel bad," does it?

By consciously changing our internal and external language or speech patterns—the words we use in talking to others and ourselves— we can transform our neural pathways, bringing us into balance and alignment with our inner and outer world. By changing our word choices, we can change the way we think and feel. Imagine the possibilities.

Sorry, I Had You on Mute

Knowing when to listen, when to talk, when to interrupt, and when to be quiet can make all the difference in the world between being a good leader and a great one.

In the 1950s, American psychologists Carl R. Rogers and Richard E. Farson[43] coined the terms "reflective listening" and "active listening" to explain a way of listening and responding that conveys

---

43 Carl R. Rogers and Richard Evans Farson, *Active Listening*, Martino, 2015.

a mutual understanding. It's listening without judgment or opinion. Practicing active listening can strengthen your awareness, improve understanding, and assist in managing conflicts. It can also bring about higher-level change in how people interact with each other.

Consider these various levels of listening:

Me (self) focus. The focus is on your thoughts, feelings, and conclusions; you can't wait until the other person stops talking so you can talk.

You (other) focus. You are focused on what the other person is saying and how they are saying it. You also pick up on what they aren't saying and notice subtle clues that reveal their emotions.

Subject focus. This is where you experience what's not being said and are involved in dialogue with complete flow, including all you see, hear, smell, and feel—all the emotional sensations. You are in a dance that results in a brilliant brainstorming session. To focus on yourself leads to mindfulness, but to focus on the internal world of others enables our neural circuitry to be harnessed, enabling us to "feel felt" by each other.

Leadership expert Simon Sinek says, "You'll be told your whole life that you need to learn to listen. I would say that you need to learn to be the last to speak." When you hold your opinions to yourself and allow others to express their views first, it does a few things.

- Creates a sense of inclusivity: Speaking last allows others to have a sense of fairness in the decision-making process.
- Weigh all viewpoints: By listening to what others say before expressing one's own views, a leader can consider all the different perspectives and opinions presented.
- Build a consensus: A leader may be able to address any remaining questions or concerns and build consensus in the group.

- More informed decisions: A leader can gather all the information, consider different perspectives, and make a more informed decision.

Meetings: Make Mine an Email, Please

Meetings are a key part of any workplace, but too often we default to a meeting when another format would work better to resolve an issue, leading to serious meeting fatigue among bosses and employees. According to Asana's The Anatomy of Work Global Index 2023[44], managers spend 58 percent of their workday on work about work (communicating about work, searching for information, switching between apps, managing shifting priorities, and chasing status updates). Meanwhile, employees waste six working weeks a year on the combination of duplicated work and unnecessary meetings: 62 percent of the workday is lost to repetitive, mundane tasks, 36 hours are spent on unnecessary meetings, and 257 hours could be saved with improved processes. **They also found that:**

- 81 percent of employees confess not paying attention or working on other tasks during a meeting.
- 45 percent of executives say that meetings serve no purpose.
- 67 percent of meetings are ineffective and unproductive.
- Too many meetings (24 percent) and uncertainty over what to prioritize (22 percent) are leading to missed deadlines.
- 23 percent of employees rate Zoom meetings as extremely exhausting.

Meetings should be a place where discussions are held and should be an opportunity for a group to make decisions. They're not a stage for the owner to prove how smart they are or to commandeer the conversation. Establishing a purpose and sticking to the timeframe and structure of meetings should be considered best practices.

---

44 https://asana.com/resources/anatomy-of-work?utm_medium=text_link&utm_source=press_release&campaign=aow24. https://asana.com/resources/anatomy-of-work

Steve Jobs was famous for holding walking meetings, which can be fruitful under the right circumstances and for a certain desired outcome. Lunch meetings serve a different purpose than coffee meetings; when you break bread with someone, you create a powerful bond and build stronger relationships. Check out the book *Death by Meetings*[45] for suggestions regarding how to structure the right format based on the purpose and outcome you are seeking.

These days, employees prefer doing skilled work and attending large meetings from home. For everything else (onboarding, one-on-one meetings, strategy/plan development, and training and development), they prefer the office. Flexible work is here to stay. With the post-pandemic shift in the ways we work, leaders must evolve, too. As the culture keepers, we need to rethink the role of the office and how hybrid opportunities will work. Even though most workers enjoy hybrid work and see the benefit of a flexible schedule, 41 percent feel more isolated working remotely. Having regular virtual or in-person events or offsites can help workers feel more connected with their colleagues. The best approach is to give agency to their employees so they are set up for success and do their best work.

My Circus, But Not My Monkeys

Do you ever feel you've spent the whole day doing everyone else's job and not yours? Are you doing more but accomplishing less? When I started my company, I was the only employee, so I had to do everything. Later on, I still tried to fix everyone else's problems myself. I could do it faster and better. I became pretty controlling.

Like most CEOs, I'm a visionary. I can see a year down the road, and all the problems, solutions, and steps to get there. I eventually learned I

---

45 Patrick Lencioni, *Death by Meeting: A Leadership Fable...About Solving the Most Painful Problem in Business*, Jossey-Bass, 2004.

had to recalibrate and reel myself back into the present moment. Going from a macro view to a micro level was hard for me. I often felt that it wasn't worth the effort it would take to explain how to get from Point A to Point Z. I see other business owners make the same mistake and it prevents them from growing to the next level.

It used to be a regular occurrence—I would arrive at my office and immediately get stopped by one of my employees, who was saying something like, "Hey, good morning. We have a problem."

I'd listen intently as they explained the situation in detail while weighing the solutions that swarmed in my head. Being wired for problem-solving, I'd get immersed in the conversation and take on the responsibility to find a fast solution: "Give me some time to think about it, and I'll get back to you."

In the book *The One Minute Manager Meets the Monkey*[46], Ken Blanchard talks about not taking about problems that aren't your own. A problem is like a monkey. In my case, the monkey was on my employee's back. While we were talking, the monkey had one leg on each of our backs. But when I said, "Let me think it over and get back to you," the monkey moved from their back to mine. Now that the monkey was firmly planted on my back, my employee walked away thirty pounds lighter.

Taking the scenario further, imagine that the next day, your employee stops by your office several times to say, "Hey, how's it coming?" Suddenly, you are feeling pressure because you haven't had time to address the problem. In my case, I not only accepted responsibility for the problem, I also promised to report back on my progress. That's fine if truly no one else can do what you do. But if the

---

46 Ken Blanchard, William Oncken Jr, and Hal Burrows, *The One Minute Manager Meets the Monkey*, William Morrow, 1999.

problem was your employee's responsibility to figure out, then you created more work for yourself.

What if someone walked up to you, handed over a newborn baby, and asked if you could figure out why it cries all the time? They tell you they will return tomorrow and check on your progress. Absurd, right? Well, it's the same thing. When you take the monkeys off people's backs, you send the message that they don't have the skills to care for and feed the monkeys themselves. You kill their initiative. Your employees are constantly asking for help because they feel dependent on you. They are afraid to make decisions.

If you repeatedly find yourself in situations in which people are trying to give their problems to you, you need to diagnose the real problem. Are you viewing your people as capable of finding solutions? Are you allowing your people to take the initiative? Or are you jumping in too quickly to save them? Do you need to learn how to let go of control and delegate effectively? Or do you need to teach your people to work and think for themselves?

Delegation can be challenging, but it's essential for effective team management and business growth. When assigning tasks, empower your employees to decide how to execute them to achieve the desired result. The learning is in the doing, which means giving your staff autonomy to make their own decisions and allowing them to learn. You have to teach them to think for themselves, even if it means cleaning up their messes for a while. It will be worth it in the long run because you will motivate them to think for themselves and take ownership of their work.

To encourage this shift in decision-making responsibility, reward your employee for their efforts, even if the outcome wasn't the best. Their first time out, it doesn't have to be perfect, because the goal is to get them comfortable with thinking on their feet. If you punish them for poor decisions, you will only train them to come back to you when there's a choice to be made, which defeats the purpose and puts more work on your plate. Instead, validate their ability to make the right choice and show them that you trust them.

If you find that your employees are still coming to you for input on tasks that require tough decisions, it may be because they are concerned about making the wrong one. Maybe they are concerned about being reprimanded, or worse. They are off the hook when they get your input. If this is happening, you haven't shown them that you trust them. You must go back and instill confidence.

You don't have to turn over the keys to the kingdom, you just have to open the door of possibilities.

It's normal for people to push back and resist a shift in ownership. It's so much easier to defer. If you are getting resistance from people you've empowered to make decisions, whatever you do, and as hard as it may be, don't continue to do the heavy lifting. Let them do the research, find a course of action, and commit to getting it done. Hold your ground and let go of any impulse you have to take control.

When delegating, consider whether the person you are delegating to has the required skills, tools, availability, and work ethic to handle the task. It is also helpful to have a positive performance history and a willingness to admit mistakes, take responsibility, and make things right. Finally, it is essential to trust and build loyalty in the person you are delegating to.

Ask them, "What do you think we should do?" If they say they don't know, remind them they are totally capable. Validate that you have the utmost confidence that they can make the right choice. Tell them, "You were hired because we know you can do this. Please come back to me with your best answer and the decision you would make, and then we will discuss." When they come back, smile, nod, and give your okay, even if they offer up an idea that you don't think will have the best outcome.

After the decision and actions have been carried out, debrief and have them share what they learned. This is an opportunity to give constructive feedback, highlighting what you liked about their performance and sprinkling in some insights about what they could do better next time. Say, "This is what I like best, and this is what I'd recommend for next time." This will help build their trust in you and confidence in themselves.

Don't revert to the old-school method of feedback—remember, hug, slap, hug? Avoid comparing their decision to what you would have done, and instead, ask yourself if the result serves the company's best interest. Be sure not to reprimand for a poor decision. Reward even those mistakes. Say something like, "I know the outcome was not what we hoped, but I'm glad you made the decision to move forward. Keep at it. It will get easier."

If you find yourself unwilling to delegate tasks because you don't think you have the time to train someone else, you are fooling yourself. That's an excuse. Delegating tasks that are not in your wheelhouse or areas of expertise or that do not utilize your time effectively can hinder the growth of your business. If you're doing anything other than what you are best at (admin stuff, entry-level activities, the minutiae), you are severely hurting the progress of your business. By continuing to do work that could be done by someone else, you are essentially doing a $15-an-hour job instead of focusing on the high-value tasks that you are skilled at and that could bring in more revenue.

As hard as it may be to let go of control, you can't do it all, and if you try, you are setting yourself up for burnout. Take the time to review your hourly, daily, and weekly tasks and take action to automate, delegate, or outsource so you can focus on what you do best, which is running the company!

When delegating, these factors are critical:

- You trust the person.
- The person instills loyalty.
- They have the necessary skills and tools.
- They have adequate availability to get the job done.
- They display a comparable work ethic to yours.
- They have a positive past performance history.
- There's a willingness to admit mistakes, take responsibility, and make things right.

The Manual Makeover

Many companies spend a lot of time documenting processes only to find that nobody cares about them or refers to them. The purpose of standard operating procedures (SOPs) is to have guidelines that will produce the same or consistent results. But creating SOPs can be tedious, especially when you are still developing systems. And when things are constantly changing, or you are growing too fast, they are even harder to maintain.

There must be an easier way to capture systems and do it seamlessly. Most companies do on-the-job training, which essentially means they wing it. This is fine when you are in a bind or heading for disaster, but it's not a long-term fix. One person has their way of doing things, and another has an alternative method. Which way is the best?

Who should design the processes? The answer is simple. It's the person already doing the work. The best way to create SOPs is to record the process as you do it. Do whatever you currently do and record it as you go. The key is to have each person capture their way of working.

Teaching is the ultimate form of learning. And when people capture the process, either through video or in writing, they retain that knowledge and prove their ability to do the task. This also prevents a gap if that person should leave suddenly, making it easy for their replacement to pick up the slack.

Are you being asked the same question over and over again? Create a system and capture the process so that it can be repeated seamlessly. The intellectual property is passed on through video or written document. As you are performing a task, record it, narrate what you are doing, and then store the video in a directory labeled with the name of the task at hand. You could have the video transcribed, so the training comes with written instructions. Store the recordings in a system that is accessible, such as a spreadsheet, to make your videos easy to find. Note that it should not take someone more than a minute to view it.

The goal is to get work off your plate and assign it to someone else to develop and improve it further. Capture what's in your head and have other people capture what they are keeping in theirs. Capture, assign, then repeat. Get everyone in the habit of regularly looking at ways to do their work more efficiently.

EXERCISE: WRONG WAY VERSUS RIGHT WAY

Below is a list of phrases that may trigger an emotional response. Say them out loud and think about how it makes you feel.

No problem.	vs.	It's all good.
No worries.		It will be fine.
I'm sick.		I don't feel well.
It's too hard.		It's not easy.
I'm nervous.		I'm excited.
It's too difficult.		It's very interesting.
I'm trying.		I'm making progress.
I forgot.		I didn't remember.
I'm starving.		I'm ready to eat.
I'm going on a diet.		I'm following a health plan.
That hurt.		That didn't feel good.

Now read the following scenarios and think about how it makes you feel. Are you motivated? Inspired? Do you feel capable of doing your job?

Scenario A

"Okay, the reason I've called you all together is to tell you just how I feel about this new project. As your boss and one of the most important members of this team, I'm feeling really anxious about our work here...uh, lack of work, that is. And I'm taking heat from the customers. It's major pressure and I'm about to go ballistic from the stress. I cannot believe how hopelessly incomplete our work has been recently. There is no way we are going to meet our deadlines. Heads are going to roll if things don't improve, and I mean now. I'm not putting up with this situation any longer. I should have known I couldn't rely on any of you to do the work it would take to get this job done. This is our fourth team meeting, and we have only one week before you are all in serious trouble."

Scenario B

"Okay, the reason I've called you all together is to tell you just how excited I am about this new project. As your boss, I'm here to support you and let you know I'm feeling really inspired about our potential with this project. I want you to understand, there will be some major pressure and sacrifices we will have to make, but I guarantee the reward will be worth it. Even though our work has been tough recently, I believe we will come together as a team and I'm confident the customer will be amazed at our ability to champion this project and deliver on schedule. This is our final push and we have a full week to deliver our promise, so let's embrace this challenge and pull off our greatest miracle ever."

What did you notice? How did you feel? Which scenario works best for you? Which boss would you rather work for?

Chapter 15
COMPETITION

*"If at first you don't succeed, try, try again. Then quit.
There's no point in being a damn fool about it." —W.C. Fields*[47]

When I started out, I enjoyed nearly zero competition in the town where my office was located. That summer, a major competitor set up shop. I found out they were a well-established company with a solid reputation. When I say well-established, I am talking about being in business for more than a hundred years. The more I found out, the more I began to fret. My future success did not look as guaranteed as I had banked on.

I will never forget the day when the supervisor of that company pulled up to my office, stepped in unannounced, walked up to my desk, and stuck his hand in my face for a handshake, obliging me to stand up. He squeezed my hand hard, looked me dead in the eye, and introduced himself as my "new competition" or "worst nightmare," something to that effect, before plopping down on my couch.

After some chitchat, he announced, "I'm here to put you out of business."

"Oh, is that right?" I was shocked by his boldness but pretended it didn't bother me. I didn't want to give him the power of seeing my fear. But I was a little shaken. I thought about it for an afternoon and

47 https://en.wikipedia.org/wiki/W._C._Fields.

came to the conclusion that the only thing I could do would be to visit my customers and ask if there was anything I could do to improve my services. I also shared my commitment to integrity and providing prompt, quality service.

It wasn't too much later that the company packed up and left town. I'm not sure what happened, whether it was because they couldn't compete with me on price or customer service, or whether the supervisor was just too cocky for his own good. I'll never know. But what I learned from that experience was the importance of understanding what your competition is doing at all times and always looking for ways that you can do your job better.

It can be challenging to have a competitor move into your market and threaten your business. I've been in other situations that didn't end in my favor. At those times, I experienced a range of emotions, from anger to envy to disgust, all of which led to some sleepless nights.

As much as it's crucial to stay aware of your competitors and understand what they are doing to make informed decisions about your own business, remember to stay true to your values and what you want to be known for. Repairing a damaged reputation is not easy. I've watched companies grow rapidly by cutting corners, lying, and cheating. But at the end of the day, what goes around comes around and they were out of business. Those nights that I couldn't sleep because I lost a major contract were painful, but having my integrity intact was worth more to me.

Taking the time to understand competitors' products or services, target market, pricing, marketing and branding, and strengths and weaknesses is valuable. Look for ways to innovate or differentiate your own business to stand out in the market and be a trailblazer.

By doing this, you can position your business for success and stay ahead of the competition.

Some things to consider when studying your competitors include:

Products or services. What do they offer, and how does it compare to what you offer? What are the key differences and similarities?

Target market. Who are your competitors targeting with their products or services? How does this compare to your target market?

Pricing. How do your competitors' prices compare to yours? Is their pricing competitive, or do they have a higher or lower price point?

Marketing and branding. How do your competitors market their products or services, and what message are they trying to convey to their target market?

Strengths and weaknesses. What are your competitors' key strengths and weaknesses? How can you leverage your own strengths to differentiate your business from them?

By understanding your competitors, you can identify opportunities to differentiate your business and make informed decisions about how to position your company in the market. But don't leave out the most important part, which is to know your customer. Understand the needs and wants of your clients and know your market. Don't make the mistake of trying to sell them something you think they want. Let your customers guide you and show you what they need.

Blazing New Goat Trails

As billionaire Sir James Goldsmith said, "If you see a bandwagon, it's already too late."[48] Innovation is the process of creating new ideas,

48 Ivan Fallon, *Billionaire: The Life and Times of Sir James Goldsmith*, Little Brown & Co., 1992.

products, or processes or improving upon existing ones. Innovation can involve introducing something completely fresh to the market or making significant improvements to an existing product or process. Innovation is often driven by a desire to solve problems, meet customer needs, or achieve competitive advantage.

Working on improving customer loyalty is one way to set yourself apart. By consistently introducing innovative products or services, you will keep your customers engaged and earn their loyalty. This will help you retain current customers as well as attract new ones.

By offering unique products or services that are in high demand, you will also benefit from increased profitability. Increasing your market share means reducing your reliance on price as a competitive advantage, which puts you in a good position to charge premium prices or attract premium clients.

Running a business takes versatility, flexibility, and guts—the kind of guts required to take risks. Nothing is ever really gained without risk and effort. Put the low-hanging fruit in your basket and focus on new ideas. Take time to develop your gut instinct for predicting trends and then figure out ways to put them into action.

Encourage your employees to think creatively, too, to come up with new ideas or more efficient ways to run the business. You will be creating a great culture and work environment, which results in better employee engagement, and likely you'll hear some imaginative suggestions that you wouldn't have come up with solo.

If innovation refers to the process of introducing new ideas, products, or processes to the market, differentiation is the special sauce full of unique features or characteristics that set you apart from your competition. Differentiation is about making a product or service stand out by highlighting its special benefits. Differentiation can be achieved through a variety of means, such as emphasizing a product's quality or performance, offering unique services, or positioning the product in a particular niche. It is often used as a marketing strategy to attract customers and distinguish a business from its competitors.

Exploring ways to differentiate involves being able to step out of your comfort zone and embrace uncertainty. Don't get me wrong, I love efficiency and processes, but don't be afraid to experiment. I wasn't growing as fast as one of my competitors, but I knew they were cutting corners—something I wasn't comfortable doing. I chose to take the slow and steady route to growth.

At the time, it was an uncomfortable choice that I kept questioning. So I looked for smaller ways to differentiate the company and create a lucrative niche.

One way to differentiate is to improve your sales and customer relations in unique ways. This takes creativity, but considering that a lot of businesses don't stay in touch with their client base or use them as a resource to find out what's missing, you can gain an advantage there. Seek suggestions not only from clients but suppliers and vendors as well. Craft a survey and poll people to find out if there is something else you can offer or do differently.

Both innovation and differentiation are essential for success in today's ever-changing, competitive marketplace. Years ago, I went to a small farmers' market at a local school. At one of the tables, I met a woman who was selling handmade soap. "Interesting," I thought, "but that will never amount to anything. How could she possibly compete with the major brands?"

Emily Voth and her husband, Todd, went on to build an empire of plant-packed home and body products now worth over $40 million. The company's differentiated focus—making their products natural and organic—was the key to the success of their company, IndigoWild[49]

---

49 https://www.indigowild.com/.

Differentiation can also be a clever marketing tool. "Where's the beef?" was a popular advertising slogan used by the fast-food chain Wendy's in 1984. A series of television commercials featured an elderly woman, Clara Peller, looking for a large, meaty hamburger patty inside a bun, with only a small amount of lettuce and tomato. The commercial ended with Clara saying the now-famous phrase, to highlight the fact that Wendy's hamburgers were made with bigger patties than those of its competitors.

The campaign was a huge success and helped to boost Wendy's sales and brand recognition. The catchphrase was widely used in popular culture, and the campaign was credited with helping to popularize the phrase "Where's the beef?" as a way of questioning the substance or quality of something.

Both innovation and differentiation are essential for businesses to stay competitive, improve customer loyalty, increase profitability, and engage their employees. Constantly seek new ways to stand out and, in turn, create value and drive success for your company over the long term.

Always Be Evolving

There is a story from the book *Art & Fear*[50] by artists David Bayles and Ted Orland that illuminates how the pursuit of quality can lead us away from success.

On the first day of class, a ceramics teacher came out and announced he would be dividing the room into two groups. He said something to the effect of, "The first group will focus on creating as much pottery as possible. If you produce fifty pounds of clay, you will get an A, forty pounds would be a B, and 30 pounds would be a C and

---

50 David Bayles and Ted Orland, *Art & Fear: Observations on the Perils (and Rewards) of Artmaking*, Image Continuum Press, 2001.

so on. For the other half of the group," he said, "I want you to focus on quality. All you need to do is create one perfect piece of pottery and I will give you an A."

At the end of the semester, when it came time for grading, the teacher determined that the group that produced the best pottery was not the one that focused on quality, but the one that focused on quantity. The quality group had spent their time theorizing on perfection, agonizing over their choices, and had little to show for their efforts.

While the quantity group was busy making as many pieces as possible, the quantity kids learned from their mistakes. As they logged in more hours of practice, they got better and better, which resulted in nearly perfect pieces. There is an important distinction between striving for perfection and striving for experience while being willing to make mistakes and learn from them. When you focus on perfection, it stunts your ability to grow.

Instead, work on continuous improvement, also known as kaizen, which is a lean business approach that involves constantly identifying and implementing small changes and improvements to increase efficiency, reduce waste, and improve quality. This philosophy encourages all members of an organization to continuously look for ways to evolve.

Continuous improvement is not a one-time event, but rather an ongoing process that involves the participation of all parties. It is a key element of Lean Management and Six Sigma and is often implemented in manufacturing and health care.

Continuous improvement helps organizations stay competitive and adapt to changing market conditions, and it can lead to increased customer satisfaction and profitability.

In a business context, continuous improvement can be applied at the individual, team, and organizational levels.

Phases of continuous improvement include:

Identifying areas for improvement. This involves pinpointing areas of the business that can be made better, such as processes, products, services, or customer experience.

Analyzing data. To make informed decisions about how to improve, businesses may need to gather and analyze data about their operations, customers, and competitors.

Implementing changes. Once areas for improvement have been identified, businesses can apply small, incremental changes to address these issues. These changes can be based on best practices, data analysis, or employee input.

Measuring results. It's important to track and measure the results of any modifications to ensure that they are effective and produce the desired outcomes.

Repeating the process. Continuous improvement is an ongoing process, so continue to look for areas for improvement, analyze data, implement changes, and measure results.

William Edwards Deming[51] was an engineer and business consultant who developed a philosophy of quality management and a cycle of continuous improvement, the four steps of which are Plan, Do, Study, and Act. He used statistics to improve quality control by examining records of defects and correcting the cause rather than reactively dealing with the symptoms. Deming believed that organizations that followed his fourteen principles would improve quality, efficiency, and customer satisfaction, and profitability. He

---

51 W. Edwards Deming, Quality Productivity and Competitive Position, MIT, 1982.

discovered that if organizations focused on boosting quality control, they would automatically reduce costs. On the other hand, if a company focused on reducing costs, it would automatically reduce quality and, paradoxically, increase costs.

At the end of World War II, Deming helped revive Japan's shattered economy. The "Made in Japan" stamp had become synonymous with cheap products, but with Deming's focus on quality control, Japan quickly became an export powerhouse, outpacing the United States by producing better and cheaper consumer goods.

When I first heard about Deming and his management principles early in my career, it had a tremendous impact. What struck me was his emphasis on the importance of getting customers and employees involved in the improvement process. When you lead people in a way that allows them to have a sense of pride in their workmanship, you get better results.

Paula Marshall, CEO of Bama Companies[52] used what she learned from Deming to shape the future of her company in ways she never imagined. Bama Companies is best known for being the single supplier of McDonald's famous Baked Apple Pie. Paula shared her CEO journey with The W. Edwards Deming Institute[53] about how she took her company from the brink of failure to thriving by going against the status quo management ideas she used. In particular, she learned the hard way how detrimental performance appraisals and incentive-based systems are to an organization.[54]

Although the philosophy of continuous improvement was developed years ago, it's still relevant today and proves there is room for flexibility and innovation in how we conduct business and manage operations.

---

52 https://www.bama.com/.
53 https://deming.org/.
54http://podcast.deming.org/paula-marshall-ceo-of-the-bama-companies-inc-discusses-her-fascinating-deming-journey.

Another way to make a significant impact is a technique known as disruptive innovation. When you disrupt the traditional ways of operating, selling, or marketing products, you shift the existing balance of market share. Think of the lightbulb, the cellphone, and Wi-Fi. Successful inventions creatively find gaps and opportunities and change traditional ways of doing business. More recent examples include cryptocurrency, rideshare services, virtual and augmented reality, 3D printing, and the Internet of Things (IoT). Disruption can cause controversy since old markets may be slow to adapt to change. The Artificial Intelligence (AI) platform ChatGPT debuted in November 2022, and just two months later, it had been banned by the nation's largest school district and was causing colleges and universities around the world to revamp how they teach.

Disruption can dramatically create new opportunities, especially when you introduce a product or service that is significantly better or cheaper than existing options or when you have an idea that has a social impact.

Purpose Over Paycheck

You will be competing for employees. The workforce is getting farther and farther away from the classic employment contract, where providing work in exchange for money is enough. More and more, people want to enjoy their job, not just make money. Purpose-driven companies are growing in popularity and changing the way we do business. They are committed to making a difference, not just profits, and look at ways to improve lives and make society and the world a better place.

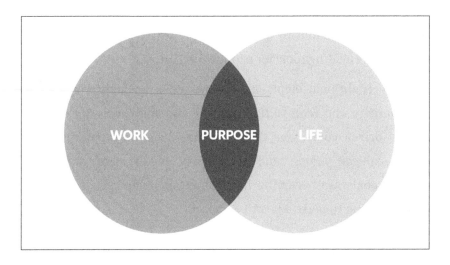

Diagram 15.1: The Art Of Living

People are looking for a balance between work and life, and a company that communicates purpose and passion to their people can benefit from increased employee retention. Making conscious and deliberate efforts to address social challenges is an honorable goal, and many companies find that it's also good for business. A recent report found consumers are 77 percent more motivated to purchase from companies committed to making the world better and 49 percent of Americans believe it's important for a company to focus on purpose over profits (Aflac CSR 2019 Survey[55]).

Here are a few of my favorite examples of socially conscious companies:

Dave's Killer Bread hires through Second Chance Employment, which means bringing employees on, regardless of criminal history.

Brooks Running, makers of quality running gear, supports diversity, equity, and inclusion (DEI) and awards grants and sponsorships to various minority and LGBTQ+ communities.

---

55 https://www.aflac.com/docs/about-aflac/csr-survey-assets/2019-aflac-csr-infographic-and-survey.pdf.

Hope Foods, which makes hummus and other dips and is based in Boulder, Colorado, aims to spread hope by breaking the silence around suicide and providing tools for people in crisis.

The traditional employment contract is no longer enough for many workers who want to find purpose and enjoyment in their jobs. Purpose-driven companies that prioritize social and environmental impact, ethical values, and community involvement along with financial goals are becoming increasingly popular and attractive to people wanting to make a positive impact.

That's why it's critical to keep your eye on the ways in which you're leading with principles and inspiration—these aren't simply sentimental ambitions but added value for your employees.

Chapter 16
CHOICES

"When you change the way you look at things, the things you look at change." —Max Planck, theoretical physicist[56]

What if I told you that intelligence is not fixed? That you have unlimited potential? All you have to do is change your belief system. Since behavior is driven by beliefs, what you believe about yourself will determine the outcome. It will also determine how motivated or driven you will be to take the action needed to get maximum results.

Belief Systems are Bs

We come into this world and must rely on our relationships for physical, emotional, and social survival. We learn to adapt to our surroundings and meet other people's expectations. We are told what's okay and what's not, what behavior gets us into trouble and what doesn't, what gets us attention, and what gets us ignored. These instructions become our brain's neural pathways. These are formed and developed through neuroplasticity, which refers to the brain's ability to reorganize and change in response to experiences and things we learn.

When we encounter new information or experiences, the brain creates new connections between neurons or strengthens existing

---

56 Max Planck, *The Origin and Development of the Quantum Theory*, Hardpress, 2012.

relationships to store and process this information. This phenomenon is especially active during early development but continues throughout life.

One way that neural pathways are developed is through repetition and practice. When we repeat an action or have a repetitive thought, the connections between the neurons involved in that action or thought become stronger. This is why it's often easier to perform a task that we have done many times compared to something new.

Neural pathways are also developed through exposure to new experiences and stimuli. When we encounter new things, our brain is challenged to make connections and learn how to process and interpret this information. Those experiences influence our perception and understanding of the world, which can lead to biases or preconceived notions that affect our ability to see objectively.

Our neural pathways become reinforced over time, and we tend to expect the present to be a certain way based on past experiences. This creates a deep groove in the neural pathways, and we are likely to keep experiencing the same results over and over. It's a thought loop, a broken record player. But we can learn to recognize and challenge our blind spots and biases by seeking fresh information and perspectives.

We can't know what we don't know. Identifying our biases requires self-awareness and a willingness to reflect on our assumptions and beliefs. Make an effort to seek out diverse perspectives and information that may challenge your views. This can involve reading books or articles, listening to podcasts or lectures, or engaging in conversations with people from different backgrounds, places, perspectives, and experiences.

Although biases are common, we all can change and grow. The key is to be open to learning and to work to recognize and challenge our personal filters. This can be a long process, but it can also be rewarding when we realize we are seeing the world as it is, rather than how we think it should be.

Hoops and Hurdles

Recently, my friend Adam called me out of the blue, leaving a message that he needed to talk. Adam came to me for coaching years ago because he couldn't understand why he didn't follow through with his goals. He felt he was constantly sabotaging his success, getting stuck in what he called hoops and hurdles. "Struggles are what's keeping me from being a success," he told me at the time. "I feel like I'm always jumping through hoops and facing hurdles. I just want to have things run smoothly for once. I want to be in a state of flow."

Getting stuck in the hoops-and-hurdles cycle happens when we are out of alignment and don't have a clear sense of purpose or direction. Alignment is that feeling of synchronicity when everything is in its right place at the right time. When we're not aligned, our subconscious fears can develop into a continuous feedback loop of never-ending doubt and anxiety. It's like a record player needle stuck in the same groove and repeats the same refrain over and over. When we spend our time focusing on what we don't want versus what we do want, fixating on problems rather than solutions, we can easily get derailed from reaching our goals.

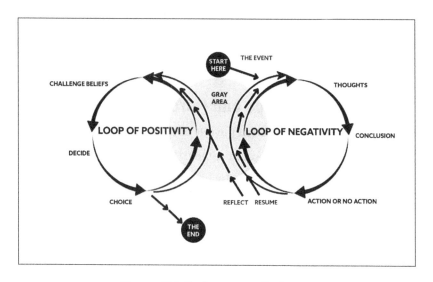

Diagram 16.1: The Constant Feedback Loop

We've all had times in our life when, no matter what we do, nothing seems to work. (It reminds me of the classic "Midvale School for the Gifted" cartoon by Gary Larson[57], in which a boy desperately pushes to enter through a door that's clearly marked "Pull.") Getting out of the hoops-and-hurdles loop will put you back in alignment.

Change is a Choice

Developmental psychologist Robert Kegan said that we humans have two primary drives, to grow and not die. But even the threat of death is often not enough to motivate us to change; only one in nine people will make a significant change even in the direst of situations. In his book *Change or Die,*[58] journalist Alan Deutschman says that facts, fears, and force simply do not work. We could prevent many outcomes by simply changing our mindset. But would you work to change your mindset when it mattered most? When your life depended on it?

---

57 Gary Larson, The Far Side Gallery, Book 1-5, Andrews McMeel, 1984.
58 Alan Deutschman, *Change or Die: The Three Keys to Change at Work and in Life*, Harper Business, 2007.

A while ago, my son took me to a rock-climbing gym for my birthday. I thought it was ironic since I'm deathly afraid of heights and had no desire to learn how to rock climb. I planned to watch him climb and be done with it.

Playing along, I had put on the rented shoes and climbed a few feet up the wall when he said, "Wait, I'll take your picture." It felt like it took him forever to get out his phone, and I was holding on for dear life when something amazing happened. By the time I came down off the wall, I felt proud that I had accomplished something significant. I had overcome my fear. I've been climbing ever since.

Climbing a wall recently, I reached a spot requiring a dynamic move. That's where you're stuck between holds, you're stretched to the max, and the only way to reach the next handhold is to push off from a foothold, leaving yourself vulnerable to losing your grip and falling. First, you must mentally commit to the moment, trust your legs' strength, create momentum, and then push off with an explosive bounce and snap, then grab the handhold above you. You don't know whether you'll be able to reach the handhold, so it comes down to trusting yourself.

It's a challenging move, especially when you're 40 feet above the ground and scared of heights. It sometimes takes every bit of energy I have, which is rewarding because I find reserves within myself that I didn't know I had. I get immense pleasure and satisfaction from conquering it.

This dynamic movement is what change feels like. Change is scary; change is uncomfortable. We like to stay in our comfort zone and focus on the stability of the foothold we have instead of looking above us for the next handhold. We get sidelined with the fear of what we will be giving up instead of thinking about what we will be gaining.

What if, instead, we thought about the satisfaction of reaching the next level? When we accept the momentum and trust the process, we invite potential and possibilities into our lives. Amazing things can happen when we surrender.

We've all experienced change. When we experience the kind of change that threatens our sense of belonging, our very survival can come into question. Social rejection lights up the same area of our brain as when we feel physical pain. It causes higher stress and emotional arousal and triggers the fear response. A threat to status can shut down the brain's capacity to see the bigger picture and prevent us from being receptive to learning, thus making it hard for people to change. No wonder we don't like change—it can be physically painful!

One thing is sure: We are forced to accept change whether we want to or not. William Bridges, author of *Transitions: Making Sense of Life's Changes*[59], says that when we're stuck between the known and the unknown, it's "as if we've launched out from a riverside dock to cross to a landing on the opposite shore—only to discover midstream that the landing was no longer there. And when we looked back at the other shore, we saw that the dock we had left from had broken loose and was heading downstream."

In my experience, change doesn't have to be hard. Let me show you what I mean. Stop what you're doing and cross your arms. Hold them there for a second. Now cross your arms in the other direction. Did it take you a couple of seconds to figure out how to do it? Did the second way feel as comfortable? If you hold the position a few seconds, it gets easier.

59 William Bridges and Susan Bridges, *Transitions (40th Anniversary Edition): Making Sense of Life's Changes*, Da Capo Lifelong Books, 2019.

History has shown us that people are resilient. We are survivors, even as each of us deals with change in our own way. Understanding that there will be a beginning, a middle, and an end can help us through even the most difficult change and uncertainty.

Change is a journey with many steps. Eckhart Tolle said it best: "Surrender is the simple but profound wisdom of yielding to, rather than opposing, the flow of life." You can't stop the world from moving forward, so be proactive and change the things you can control, among them yourself.

Here are some mindset shifts to consider:

Be flexible, adaptable, and embrace change. When water is prevented from flowing, it becomes stagnant. Only what's dead doesn't grow.

Be proactive by practicing awareness and moment-to-moment living. Do the things that put you in the zone, such as art, dance, cooking, listening or creating, music, reading, writing, and more.

Be accountable for your health and wellness. Assess where you are and where you'd like to be. What's preventing you from making changes?

Practice acceptance. Not accepting change is like sailing through life without raising the anchor. Let go of regrets and grudges. Forgiveness is life changing.

Plan for happiness. Take time to reflect and create meaning in your life by finding ways to honor your values.

Alan Deutschman, inspired by a Clint Eastwood line in Heartbreak Ridge— "You improvise, you adapt, and you overcome."—developed the following **Three Keys to Change:**[60]

1. **Relate.** Find a person or community that inspires and sustains hope.

2. **Repeat.** Learn, practice, and master new habits and skills.

3. **Reframe.** Cultivate new ways of thinking about your situation and your life.

Here is my strategy, based on my business experience, to inspire you to become your own change agent and life entrepreneur:

1. Design and build a new plan.

2. Identify what needs to happen to lead to success.

3. Create a process to move in the right direction.

4. Identify stumbling blocks and hoops and hurdles you may run into.

5. Recognize opportunities and act on them.

6. Trust your gut and find resilience in the face of adversity.

7. Test for target accuracy.

8. Redirect course and take action.

9. Monitor results and adjust if necessary.

By changing our mindset, we could avoid many pitfalls. It takes courage to take your foot off the ledge and jump to the next level. By taking proactive steps to engineer your life and trusting the process, you will be amazed at what you accomplish.

---

60 Alan Deutschman, The Three Keys to Change, Fast Company, January 01, 2007, https://www.fastcompany.com/75905/three-keys-change.h

There are several reasons why businesses should embrace change:

To stay competitive. Businesses adapting to changing market conditions and customer needs are more likely to thrive and remain competitive. Embracing change can help businesses stay ahead of the curve and respond to new opportunities and challenges.

To improve efficiency and productivity. Businesses can increase efficiency and productivity by continuously improving processes and adopting new technologies. This can help them save time, reduce costs, and increase profitability.

To foster innovation and creativity. Change can encourage employees to think outside the box and develop innovative solutions to problems. This can lead to new products or services, which can help businesses stay relevant and attract new customers.

To adapt to regulatory changes. Businesses operating in regulated industries may be required to make changes to comply with new regulations or laws. Embracing these changes can help businesses avoid legal consequences and maintain a good reputation.

To attract and retain talent. Many employees value a work environment open to innovation. By embracing change, businesses can attract and retain top talent, which can help them succeed in the long run.

If you are the leader implementing change(s), you'll need support in doing so in the most positive and least disruptive way possible.

Leadership and business expert Dr. Mary Lippitt's model for Managing Complex Change includes five components:

1. **Vision.** Communicate why you are making the change.
2. **Skills.** Make sure people are prepared.
3. **Incentives.** Offer rewards, recognition, and celebrations.
4. **Resources.** Have the money, time, and equipment needed.
5. **Action Plan.** Incorporate a plan broken into steps to accomplish the details.

Say you want to implement new processes for onboarding recruits. If you fail to address or communicate any one of these five components, you could face confusion, anxiety, and frustration, and you may fail to get the job done or make the changes.

To paraphrase a line from the movie Moneyball[61], the person who smacks the ball over the fence is the one who steps up to the plate with a heart full of conviction and determination. Nobody ever made a home run who was afraid of the pitcher.

As I've stated, the goal with my company was to always know what my competition was doing so I could stay one step ahead. The way to accomplish that was to evolve and look for ways to differentiate my product or services. This strategy means being painfully aware that change is constant. As a CEO, if you aren't prepared to deal with change, then you will probably not survive.

One way to train your mind to accept flexibility and resilience is by engaging the reticular activating system (RAS), a network of neurons in the brainstem that plays a key role in regulating arousal and attention. The RAS receives input from various sensory systems and sends output to the cerebral cortex, which is the part of the brain responsible for conscious thought and decision-making. It's like your own personal search engine. It can filter out eight million bits of subconscious information by simply focusing on a few keystrokes or words. Suppose you are looking for your car keys. The RAS may filter out unrelated stimuli and focus your attention on potential key hiding places.

The RAS is also involved in sleep and wakefulness, and it helps to regulate the release of certain neurotransmitters. Things like dopamine and norepinephrine play a role in arousal and alertness. If you've ever been sound asleep, but you woke up at the slightest noise your baby made, that's the RAS kicking in.

---

61 Michael Lewis, *Moneyball: The Art of Winning an Unfair Game*, W.W. Norton & Company, 2003.

Neuroscience tells us RAS can be used to manage stress and achieve success, too. You can train your RAS by setting clear goals, prioritizing tasks, and focusing on positive and empowering thoughts. Have you ever started thinking about something and suddenly started seeing it everywhere? You want a dog, and now everyone seems to have one. Your brain is like a little puppy, willing to do whatever you request. That's why it's so important to be aware of what you're thinking. If you ask negative questions, such as, Why am I broke? Why can't I make money? The RAS will help you find the evidence you are looking for to support those thoughts.

Instead, switch from finding fault to finding solutions. Inspirational business expert Anthony J. D'Angelo[62] says it best: "Wherever you go, no matter what the weather, always bring your own sunshine."

Manage The Why, Not Time

Our priorities can change in an instant. We can go from being too busy to take a lunch break to getting a phone call that our house is on fire and then dropping everything. Time management is choice management. Time management is priority management. It can take a long time to finish something that you aren't working on. When someone tells you they don't have the time, what they are telling you is that they don't want to do something.

While it makes sense that we have to wear all the hats when our businesses are getting off the ground, it's not sustainable as we grow. Ask yourself, would my life be easier if my team members were empowered to make decisions and I felt confident that their decisions would routinely grow and sustain the business?

---

62 Anthony J. D'Angelo, Dan Oltersdorf, Amy Connolly, *Inspiration for Resident Assistants*, The Collegiate Empowerment Company, 2001.

Is your goal for things to get more chaotic, or do you want things to run smoothly? If you answered smoothly, of course, then it's worthwhile to design a time management plan.

The Must-Haves

This is the activity involved in working on the business. Spend time evolving and strategizing to stay ahead of the competition or develop differentiators that will bring in more business. You are the architect, the designer who is thinking strategically, staying several steps ahead, and measuring the risk and opportunities. Think of ways to simplify processes to get the same or better results than in the past, with less effort.

If you say your business can't be streamlined and it can't run without you, you are lying to yourself. I believe every business can be systematized. In most cases, it's the owner that doesn't know how to systemize and is too embarrassed to admit it. This is where it's important to go through an analysis of where you are spending most of your time.

Take note of which tasks do not benefit the company or the revenue goal and which tasks distract you from doing work that matters.

The Must-Do's

These are the tasks you love to do and are essential because they bring you the most joy. Don't give these to anyone else. For the things you must keep, evaluate how they can be trimmed, done faster, or more efficiently.

This is the necessary work and the activities that serve clients and maintain operations. This is where most startups start—but also where most get stuck indefinitely if they cannot learn to let go.

The Must-Decides

This is the process of making choices and deciding what tasks to assign to what people. If you assign a task to someone else but need to answer questions to get the job done, you are not delegating. You are deciding for them. Just because you are doing something doesn't mean it's something you should be doing. Most companies become inefficient because the owner doesn't realize that other people are waiting on them to make decisions. Transfer work down to the most inexpensive resource and empower the new task owner to achieve the intended outcome more effectively. The only true failure is failure to decide.

The Must-Drops

Get rid of the things that are not necessary. What are the tasks you can automate, delegate, or outsource? Unsubscribe from everything. As the saying goes, some tasks are better deleted than completed.

A good rule of thumb is 80/20: Block out at least 80 percent of your time on the calendar to focus on those tasks that have the highest impact on your business, add the most value, and will produce the most income. These are the things that no one else can do as well as you. The other 20 percent of your time should be spent on administrative tasks, planning the use of resources and schedules for the operations, and developing ways to improve performance.

Dividing your tasks into four categories—must have, must do, must decide, and must drop—will help you better allocate your time. Let go of tasks that distract from doing work that matters and will empower team members to make decisions and take on tasks to sustain the business.

Competing Commitments

It's easy to see why so many people are resistant to change. Getting out of our comfort zone and learning new tasks, working with new team members, or being challenged in a new position can be scary. It can be daunting and lonely at the top. Leaders can get caught up in trying to maintain a certain status, afraid to show any hint of weakness or vulnerability. That's because we feel threatened when our status is threatened. That's also why people go to extreme lengths to win arguments—to prove they are right. We think being wrong reduces our status while increasing the other person's, and losing social status is among the most terrible consequences we can imagine.

Even if we understand logically that it can be tough to make big shifts, it's still endlessly frustrating to experience it in others and ourselves. We all know people who tell you they are intent on doing things differently but just keep dragging their feet. Sometimes you know what you need to do, but you seem to sabotage your own efforts. Stop spending time pushing a boulder up a hill only to watch it roll back down. It has to do with something called "competing commitments."

In their book *Immunity to Change,* organizational psychologists Robert Kegan and Lisa Lashkow Lahey[63] explain that even when we are committed to change, we often unwittingly put more energy toward a hidden, competing commitment. This stalls our efforts to work towards a goal. It's a "personal immunity to change."

During a recent conversation, the membership director of a businesswomen's organization who had reached out about speaking to their group mentioned that she was having difficulty getting things accomplished. After we talked for a while, it was evident that she was

---

63 Robert Kegan et al., *Immunity to Change: How to Overcome It and Unlock the Potential in Yourself and Your Organization,* Harvard Business Review Press, 2009.

struggling with deciding between two competing priorities: work life and family life. She wanted to grow her business, which would require her to work harder and put in more overtime hours, but she also wanted to spend more time with her family and was feeling pressured to do so. Her commitment to her business and her commitment to her family were competing for her time.

So how do we go about uncovering competing commitments? This awareness may lie deep in our subconscious and take time to figure out. The psychological foundations may be difficult to explore, especially in a work environment. But by asking the right questions, you can prevent potentially embarrassing situations and create powerful and lasting change.

Here are some questions that will help uncover the competing commitment:

What's your goal? What are you committed to? What would you like to see changed? If you ask these questions to a staff member, recognize that they may raise a complaint, such as "I'd have more time to do my work if I didn't always have to check her work for mistakes" or "I am feeling overwhelmed learning the new system." Complaints are useful, as people tend to complain about what they care about.

What commitment do you have that is not fully recognized by this situation? In every complaint, there is the value of what's not being honored. Unlock the underlying value to find a clue as to what needs to be done to create meaningful change.

What are you doing or not doing that is keeping your commitments from being realized? This question aims to identify and understand why people behave in ways that undermine their own success.

What will happen if you do the opposite? Would you experience discomfort, worry, or fear? This question explores the consequences of the behavior.

By engaging in undermining behavior, what worrisome outcome are you committed to preventing? The answer is the competing commitment that lies at the heart of why people don't change.

What is the big assumption you are making that validates your perception? This question uncovers deep-rooted beliefs about ourselves and the world around us. It reveals how the competing commitment arises from the big assumption as a form of self-protection.

Here's an example of how you can frame your competing commitment dilemma. Fill in the blanks with a conflict you've encountered recently, such as you want to do X but you find yourself doing Y.

THE GAS	THE CHOICE	THE CONFLICT	THE BRAKES
The goal (Statement: I am committed to...)	What am I doing or not doing (behavior) that keeps me from my commitments and achieving my goals?	I'm also committed to... (the competing commitment)	Big assumptions
Get my Series 6 license.	I want to spend more time with my family.	My family needs me and my husband is providing.	I assume I will lose my connection to my family if I am working too hard.
Build a team.	I can't find the right market and don't know how.	I don't have the confidence I need to get in front of the right people.	The license will give me the confidence.

Once you've identified your assumptions, you want to challenge them. See if you can adopt a different perspective. Challenging your beliefs and assumptions can be disorienting. In fact, doing so is sometimes called a "disorienting dilemma," a term developed by Jack Mezirow in his book *Transformative Learning in Practice*[64].

When new information is presented, it can force us to question our values, beliefs, or assumptions, leading to transformational learning. This can be caused by an unexpected event that throws us for a loop, or maybe we are sick and tired of being sick and tired and decide we need to change. By working through this process, you can learn to identify inner conflicts, overcome blind spots, and achieve goals more effectively. There is a big upside to working towards this self-awareness.

Embrace the teaching moments of mistakes and failure. Be vulnerable, elicit change, and find peace in the moment. Challenge your assumptions and beliefs so you can reach a new level and a new normal, working towards your peak potential and being in alignment with your higher purpose.

Getting Unstuck with a Mindset for Success

Mindset is your way of thinking, or you could say it's your attitude. In more technical terms, mindset is a series of self-perceptions and beliefs you hold about yourself and others. And since thoughts influence our mood and our moods are the emotions we feel, mindset is important to understand.

Research has shown that a person's mindset can play a significant role in determining an individual's outcome in life. Becoming aware of your mindset, understanding why you do or think the things you do,

---

64 Jack Mezirow and Edward W. Taylor, *Transformative Learning in Practice: Insights from Community, Workplace and Higher Education*, Jossey-Bass, 2009.

and learning how to adapt and shift your way of thinking can greatly improve your health, decrease stress, and make you more resilient to life's challenges.

Our state of mind is also influenced by the interactions and relationships we have with others. The strongest emotion in the room can ripple out and elicit the same feeling in others without anyone's conscious awareness.

The right mindset can have a powerful interpersonal effect and even cause us to release the hormone oxytocin, which alleviates fear and enhances learning and development. We relate well with people from whom we "catch" emotions that benefit us. These "attuned" relationships are vital to health and wellness, and, no doubt, qualities such as integrity, passion, and courage attract and retain the best of the best of the workforce.

On the flip side, when we get attached to being comfortable, complacent, and right, we don't question what we don't perceive, just as we don't think about taking our next breath. We make unfortunate assumptions to make us feel better about ourselves or complement our personal perspectives.

Developing more positive mindsets, such as a growth mindset, can greatly improve our quality of life, help us reach our goals, and set us up for success. Your mindset impacts your life, so it's important that you cultivate the right one.

Stanford University psychology professor Carol Dweck[65] developed mindset theory in the 1970s by observing children and the stark differences in how they handled adversity or setbacks. She noticed that some children were averse to challenges while others sought them out. She suggests that fixed and growth mindsets live by different rules.

---

65 Carol S. Dweck PhD, *Mindset: The New Psychology of Success*, Random House, 2006. https://www.youtube.com/watch?v=isHM1rEd3GE.

In a fixed mindset:
- People strive to appear talented to others.
- They believe they shouldn't have to work hard; they were good at things when they were younger and they don't feel that need to push themselves now.
- They do what they can to hide their weakness from others, and they don't risk doing anything that will show their weaknesses or attempt to learn anything new if they think they may fail.

In a growth mindset:
- People strive to learn.
- They work with passion and dedication and strive to give their best effort. They had to struggle and work hard for success, and they learned that effort matters and they can always improve their skill.
- They are not afraid of failure and aim to improve, even if they will appear weak or silly.

No one person is 100 percent one or the other, but it's beneficial to try to move toward the growth mindset side of the continuum. That's because a positive mindset supports our overall well-being.

According to the Mayo Clinic[66], the health benefits of a positive mindset include:
- Increased life span
- Lower rates of depression
- Lower levels of distress and pain
- Greater resistance to illnesses
- Better psychological and physical well-being
- Better cardiovascular health and reduced risk of death from cardiovascular disease and stroke

---

66 Dana Sparks, Mayo Mindfulness: Overcoming Negative Self-Talk, Mayo Clinic News Network, May 29, 2019. https://newsnetwork.mayoclinic.org/discussion/mayo-mindfulness-overcoming-negative-self-talk/

Having an entrepreneurial or growth mindset is worthwhile in all aspects of life. It's useful when navigating day-to-day challenges. It helps you adapt and cope with rapid change and uncertainty. It supports academic and career success. Next time something negative happens to you or you feel yourself labeling it as a negative experience, try to see the positive in the situation. Your mind is a powerful thing when you fill it with positive thoughts; your life and your outlook on life will start to be transformed for the better.

Jumping to Conclusions

In the movie *Office Space*, one of the characters talks about his million-dollar idea of selling a "jumping to conclusions" mat. He tries to sell his idea to his colleagues: "It's a mat that you would put on the floor, and it would have different conclusions written on it that you could jump to." It sounds silly, but we do it all the time. All of us tend to rely on our subconscious filters and mental maps, which were instilled in our subconscious long before we could reevaluate or process them. We spend most of our day on autopilot, making judgments and disregarding information that doesn't fit our mindset, which is based on those subconscious beliefs or conditioning. Bruce Lipton[67], a renowned developmental biologist, says, "Our thoughts are mainly controlled by our subconscious, which is largely formed before the age of six, and you cannot change the subconscious mind just by thinking about it. That's why the power of positive thinking will not work for most people. The subconscious mind is like a tape player. Until you change the tape, it will not change." Trusting our assumptions is like believing in fortune cookies; it's entertaining, but it's not based in reality nor is it relevant to the situation.

---

67 Bruce Lipton, *The Biology of Belief: Unleashing the Power of Consciousness, Matter, and Miracles*, Hay House, 2016.

Practicing awareness can be no less challenging than juggling flaming torches. In fact, it's rather unnerving. We get attached to being comfortable and complacent, and our mind finds ways to prove we are right. When other people disagree with us, we think 1) they must be ignorant, 2) they are major idiots, and 3) maybe they are just evil. We jump to conclusions because we must protect what we believe is true— at all costs!

EXERCISE: STOP PLAYING WHACK-A-MOLE

Do you ever feel like there's never enough time in the day? Do you feel like you are constantly playing whack-a-mole with problems and tasks? Grab your notebook. This time-management quiz will help you get clear on what matters most in the areas of goal setting, prioritization, handling interruptions, procrastination, and scheduling. It will also reveal key points of what's keeping you from being effective and efficient. Answer the following statements with never, rarely, sometimes, often, or always.

1. Setting goals helps me decide what tasks and activities I should work on.
2. I consistently track my progress when I set new goals.
3. I am stressed out about deadlines and commitments.
4. I find myself dealing with interruptions.
5. With every new task or project, I analyze its importance and prioritize accordingly.
6. Distractions keep me from working on critical tasks.
7. I have to take work home (or work after hours) to get it done.
8. I find myself completing tasks at the last minute or asking for an extension.
9. I set aside personal focus time for planning and scheduling.
10. I leave contingency time in my schedule to deal with the unexpected.
11. The tasks I spend the most of my time on are the ones with the highest impact and are the highest-revenue-producing activities.
12. I know how much time I spend on the various tasks I do.
13. I rate the tasks I'm working on based on high, medium, or low value.
14. I have a to-do list or action plan that I refer to often.

15. Before I take on a task or project, I confirm that the time spent will be worth the results I get.

16. I regularly confirm my staff is focused on their highest priorities.

17. I spend too much time in unproductive meetings, responding to unimportant emails, or returning important phone calls while driving.

18. I'm often fixing problems for others or doing things other people should be doing.

19. There is confusion among my staff about what should be done and when.

20. My workspace is organized and uncluttered. I don't spend a lot of time searching for things.

Look at your answers and refer to the insights and questions below to promote self-knowledge and get yourself on track.

QUESTIONS 1–3: SETTING GOALS

The key to success is knowing where you are and where you are going. Setting goals will reduce confusion and help you manage your time effectively. Without clarity of your goals and objectives, you will be in a constant mode of reacting to problems without planning or foresight. Being predictive is better. With a proactive approach, you anticipate possible scenarios and take steps to prepare for them in advance.

QUESTIONS 4–7: MANAGING INTERRUPTIONS

Work to minimize interruptions. Maybe you need to learn how to say no. Say no to unnecessary tasks or commitments so you can free up your time for more important things. Set aside daily focus time for yourself and stick to it. Take breaks to improve your focus and productivity.

Set boundaries by making yourself available to people on your schedule. Audit what you are doing that causes you to fall behind, and identify your weaknesses. Do you have more trouble delegating, managing interruptions, or deleting unnecessary tasks?

QUESTION 8: PROCRASTINATION

Evaluate the minutiae you are dealing with every day to prevent procrastination. Consider doing the hardest tasks first, rewarding yourself with easier tasks for the rest of the day. If you consistently have trouble with procrastination, there could be an underlying issue that's causing resistance. Consider other factors that may be preventing you from acting. Are you unmotivated? Do you lack structure and accountability? Are you a perfectionist and fear failure?

QUESTIONS 9–10: SCHEDULING/CALENDAR BLOCKING

Learn how to effectively schedule your time. Calendar blocking is very effective for some people, and others can't stick to routines or the commitment it requires. The most critical thing is to stay organized and on top of your responsibilities, so whatever type of system you use, make sure it's the best for you. Schedule priority tasks and leave a little wiggle room for interruptions and unexpected events.

QUESTIONS 11–15: PRIORITIZATION

Without prioritization, you may work hard but won't achieve desired results. To work efficiently, work on the highest-value tasks first. To-do lists are great, but without prioritization, you may be wasting time. Prioritize your list based on the importance and urgency of the task. Put less important tasks on the back burner. Structure your work ahead of time to ensure you get the best results. Consider using a timer to stay on track.

QUESTIONS 16–19: DELEGATION

Structure your work ahead of time to ensure you get the best results. Look for ways to delegate your most unproductive tasks. Getting clear on how to delegate effectively can save you time and effort. Helping your staff become more efficient will also help you become more efficient and minimize interruptions. Work toward having brief daily or weekly check-ins or track KPIs (key performance indicators) with staff to ensure they are focused on the right things.

QUESTION 20: ORGANIZATION

Creating processes and systems will get you more organized. Review your progress and adjust as needed. Be adaptable and willing to make changes, and be open to trying different strategies. The more focused time you spend organizing your day, the greater the impact on your life.

EXERCISE: DO THE 180

Challenging your automatic thoughts and assumptions takes time. Still, with practice, you can become more aware of the random, unchallenged thoughts in your head. Blaze new trails and create opportunities for yourself by taking "what is" and asking "what could be?" There isn't an easy answer to why we do what we do, but that's okay. We all do the best we can, and we are all a work in progress. But we can never begin to know what we don't know if we don't challenge our assumptions. Instead, we lose ourselves to the mundane, time-bound world where we go about our day on autopilot, managing the barriers and constrictions of schedules, deadlines, and responsibilities. The way to keep from making assumptions is to ask questions.

Here is a tool to help you start questioning your basic assumptions. If we put this tool into daily practice, we will become more aware of illogical or irrelevant assumptions we make automatically.

Type into an Excel sheet or use a blank piece of paper to write out three columns with the headings Observe, Assess, and Rework. The OAR can be just the paddle you need to get you up a creek.

OBSERVE	ASSESS	REWORK
Joe is defensive and difficult to get along with.	Joe reminds me of my crazy Uncle Harry, who I could never stand being around.	My coworker could be a nice guy. I will spend time getting to know him without judging him so quickly.

Take a minute to think about a difficult situation you are currently dealing with. For example, you are having trouble getting along with someone you work with. You find them irritating, defensive, and insubordinate.

First column: Write down the behavior or emotion and then sit back and observe it with detachment, as if you were in the balcony watching actors on stage. What assumptions are you making about the other person and the situation? Is it true? What if it were not true? What if the person in your department were not defensive or difficult to get along with? Maybe he reminds you of your less-than-favorite crazy Uncle Harry?

Second column: Write down your thoughts as you question the statement's validity. Maybe you are overgeneralizing or making an assumption based on an irrational belief: "I never really gave my coworker a chance because of the way he looked and how that triggered my association with Uncle Harry."

Third column: This is the 180—the reframing or adjustment of the statement with your new understanding, which is a new reality statement: "My co-worker could be a nice guy; I will spend time getting to know him without judging him so quickly."

FINAL NOTE

You made it! Congratulations.

You've explored the multi-faceted world of entrepreneurship and leadership through the lens of the Middle Way approach. You've journeyed through the financial superpowers to expand profit margins, carved your unique leadership path, embraced the essence of people and culture, and understood the fundamentals of efficient business processes. As we reflect, let's encapsulate the lessons learned and offer guidance on your ongoing journey.

In Part One, we unearthed the potent power of finances. We learned not to fear numbers but to wield them as tools in the quest for business success. Remember always to have a keen eye on cash flow, capital, costs, and capacity. Stay prepared for the unpredictable future, and keep on learning and adapting your financial strategies.

Part Two reminded us that leadership isn't about exerting control but about paving the way for others to shine. It's about having the courage to face challenges head-on and fostering an environment that breeds creativity and innovation. Continue to work on self-awareness, face your fears, and foster an innovative culture. Remember, leadership is a journey, not a destination.

Part Three emphasized the importance of people in our business. The success of your venture lies not only in the strength of your idea but also in the strength of your team. Strive to create a strength-based culture, foster collaboration, manage conflicts skillfully, and attract and retain the best talent. Your business is as strong as your team, so ensure they feel valued, heard, and understood.

In Part Four, we honed the critical skills needed to run an efficient business operation. Emphasize open communication, understand the role of competition, and make conscious and informed choices. Don't underestimate the impact of a positive, success-oriented mindset—it's the engine that will keep your business moving forward.

Finally, keep the 'Twelve Principles of Middle Way Leadership' close to your heart. These principles will guide you to strike a delicate balance between challenges and opportunities, instilling within you the key characteristics of successful entrepreneurship.

This book's journey might be at an end, but your journey as an entrepreneur is just beginning or advancing into its next chapter. Remember, the road to success is often paved with failures. It's not about the number of times you fall but the number of times you get up, learn, and move forward. The Middle Way Leader isn't just a title—it's a mindset. Carry it with you as you conquer your dreams, and you'll find yourself thriving, not just surviving.

Here's to your continued journey of growth, success, and resilience. Remember to revisit these lessons and principles as you navigate your path and always strive to embody the Middle Way Leader. May you lead with heart, wisdom, and strength—ever forward, ever upwards.

APPENDIX A:
BUILD YOUR P&L FROM SCRATCH

The P&L statement will show you the amount of revenue and expenses the company has earned over time. You want to get in the habit of tracking this information over the long haul so you can gain insight into the bigger picture.

For example, when you look at month-to-month comparisons, you may find that your expenditures rise and fall in certain months. With this knowledge, you can better prepare your budget. Besides month-to-month, you will also want to track quarterly and annual numbers.

We will need to know:

- Revenue
- COGS (variable costs)
- Overhead (fixed costs).

These are the only three numbers you really need to focus on. The reason they are so important has to do with the simple fact that these three are the only numbers in your P&L that you can directly impact.

These are the steps you'll need to take to complete your P&L:

Bank statements. The first step is to gather your previous bank statements or obtain as many as you can, preferably twelve months of statements, but any amount will work for this exercise.

Revenue. Next, add up all of the business-related deposits you made during that time frame. The total is your revenue.

COGS. Now, add up all of your business-related expenses (withdrawals on your bank statement) and go through those expenses line item by line item. COGS are those direct costs you incur to deliver your product or service, meaning expenses that are directly connected to a specific product. These include direct and contractual labor, materials, packaging, distribution, shipping, and sales commissions.

Overhead. These are the costs you incur, regardless of whether you sell anything. Overhead are those indirect expenses involved in running and maintaining your company. These include costs such as rent, insurance, utilities, office supplies, office personnel salaries, general maintenance, advertising, janitorial costs, and auto expenses.

Fill out your P&L. Finally, from the numbers you were able to get from the categories above, record everything on the P&L in the appropriate columns. Once you have these numbers, you can do the calculations for the other numbers (gross and net profit) that will be valuable for you to know.

APPENDIX B:
THE BEST MARKETING BANG
FOR YOUR BUCK

Let's look at two different strategies when working with a marketing budget. This highlights that the more you spend doesn't always equate to the more you get.

Plan A

Let's say you are a financial planner and have been considering online pay-per-click advertising. You want to build your book of business and get attendees to the webinar you want to host. The first thing you need to understand is the lifetime value you'll receive from your average client. A simple formula is:

Customer Lifetime Value = Average Total Spend Amount ×
Average # of Purchases Per Year × Retention Rate

If your average client spends $200 per month and stays with you for two years, the customer lifetime value would be: $200 × 12 × 2 = $4,800.

Let's start with an advertising budget of $2,000 for Google pay-per-click (PPC) ads, with an average PPC of $2.32. When a prospect clicks on our ad, Google deducts $2.32 from your $2,000 monthly budget.

Next, let's calculate the number of clicks we can expect based on our budget. To do this, we divide $2,000 by $2.32 and get 862 clicks.

Google and Facebook track ads and know the average number of conversions generated by ads similar to yours. Suppose this number is 7.21 percent. Let's multiply our 862 expected clicks by 7.21 percent (which in decimal form is 0.0721) and find that we can expect to generate 62 prospects for our ad.

The average percentage of those prospects attending the webinar is around 40 percent. If we plan for the worst and assume only 25 percent will attend, this reduces the potential prospects to only 15 (by rounding up).

Now we can estimate a conservative close rate of 15 percent for the people in attendance. In that case, we can estimate the number of new clients our webinar should generate by multiplying 15 attendees by 15 percent, which equals two new clients.

With this information, we can now determine if the marketing ad will be profitable by considering its lifetime value. If we get two clients worth $4,800 lifetime value and multiply those two numbers, our total gross profit from our ad campaign will be $9,600.

If we subtract our advertising cost of $2,000, we will see a net profit of $7,600. If you take the net profit of $7,600 and divide it by the amount you spent, $2,000, you get a 380 percent return on investment (ROI). This scenario is ideal!

$$7600 \div 2000 \times 100 = 380\% \text{ ROI}$$

Plan B

Plan A appears to be working out well. What would happen if you spent double the money on ads? Wouldn't you get even better results? Let's find out.

Let's double our monthly advertising budget of $2,000 to $4,000, and double our click costs from $2.32 to $4.64 because Google will rank us higher and more customers will be able to find us. The number of clicks we expect to generate would stay the same at 862.

Let's take a conservative approach and cut our webinar conversion rate in half from 7.21 percent to just 3.61 percent. We multiply the conversion rate of 3.61 percent by our 862 clicks and we predict we would get 31 attendees.

Again, we can leave the attendance percentage at 25 percent. That means only seven will attend out of the 31 prospects registered. Keeping our closing rate at 15 percent, we can expect to generate just one new client. Our new client has a lifetime value of $4,800. If we subtract our $4,000 ad cost, we have a net profit of $800. That's only a 20 percent return on investment—much less than we'd expect by doubling our contribution.

$$800 \div 4000 \times 100 = 20\% \text{ ROI}$$

We understand that marketing can be the go-to solution for many business owners looking to increase revenue and profit. However, as we've shown in this exercise, it's not always the best answer. In fact, marketing campaigns often fall short when it comes to boosting profit.

That's why we recommend implementing the strategies we've covered first, and then consider a campaign to further increase revenue. Once you've done that, if you decide that Google or Facebook is the right platform to reach your target audience, the formulas for lifetime value and return on investment will ensure the success in your approach. Remember to set realistic expectations and track your progress over time to evaluate the success of your marketing efforts.

APPENDIX C:
GLOSSARY

Accrual basis accounting: Records income when the transaction takes place and records expenses when you receive the bill. Uses advanced accounting, such as accounts payable. Tracks long term liabilities, loans, and inventory. Larger businesses are required by the IRS to use an accrual basis.

Benchmarking: How your business is trending compared to your competitors and industry leaders.

Bottom-line growth: Growing earnings and reducing costs.

Cash basis accounting: Records expenses when you pay and income when you receive it. Tracks cash, expenses, and income. Does not track long term liabilities, loans, and inventory. There are size restrictions for which companies can use the cash basis.

COGS (Cost of goods sold): The total of all the costs used to create a product or deliver a service, which has been sold.

EBITA: Also known as "earnings before interest and taxes and amortization." A 60 percent margin in most industries would be considered excellent.

Forecasting: Making predictions based on historical data and the current situation.

Gross profit: The money left over after the company's costs are deducted from sales.

Gross margin: The company's gross profit divided by its sales, which represents the amount earned in profit per dollar of sales.

Gross profit margin: Higher gross profit margins indicate the company is efficiently converting its product (or service) into profits. The cost of

APPENDIX D:
CALCULATIONS

Assets = Liabilities + Equity

Break-Even Point = Fixed Costs ÷ (Sales Price per Unit – Variable Costs per Unit)

Cash Flow to Debt Ratio = (Net Income + Depreciation) ÷ Total Debt

COGS = (Cost of Goods Sold) is the total of all the costs used to create a product or deliver a service, which has been sold.

Equity = Assets – Liabilities

Gross Margin = Revenue – Variable Expenses

Gross Profit = Revenue – COGS

Gross Profit Margin Percentage = Gross Profit ÷ Revenue × 100

Net Income = Revenue – Expenses

Net Profit = Gross Profit – Overhead

Net Profit Margin Percentage = Net Profit ÷ Revenue × 100

Net Sales = Revenue – Returns, Discounts, and Sales Allowances

Operating Cash Flow = Operating Income + Depreciation – Taxes + Change in Working Capital

Operating Profit Margin = Gross Profit – Operating Expenses ÷ Revenue × 100

Profit = Sales Revenue – Total Costs

Profit per Job = Profit ÷ Transactions

Revenue per Employee = Annual Sales or Revenue ÷ Total Employees

Revenue ÷ Average Sale = # of Transactions

Revenue Goal ÷ Average Job Size Goal = # of New Projects Goal

ROI = Net Profit ÷ Shareholder's Equity

Seasonality = Monthly Sales ÷ Total Sales for the Year

goods sold is the total amount to produce a product, including materials and labor. Margins in the consulting world can be 80 percent to 100 percent, whereas a restaurant may have a razorthin 3 to 5 percent margin.

Net profit margin: Higher net profit margins show that the company is efficiently converting sales into profit. Look at similar companies to benchmark success as net profit margins will vary by industry. A 20 percent margin is considered high/good, 5 percent is low, and 10 percent is average.

Pro forma: A document with hypothetical data or assumptions used to predict future performance.

Return on investment (ROI): Often used to measure performance and to evaluate the efficiency or outcome of an investment.

Revenue: The total amount of sales recognized for a specific reporting period, prior to any deductions.

Top-line growth: Increased revenue ÷ gross sales.

APPENDIX E:
KEY PERFORMANCE INDICATORS (KPIS)

A KPI can be anything. It doesn't have to be a number. Here's a list of KPIs in specific categories to give you an idea of what you could be tracking in your company.

Company Level

- Revenue
- MRR (monthly recurring revenue)
- Revenue per hour/day/week
- Revenue per client
- Revenue per stream (product or service)
- Expenses
- Cash on hand
- AP/AR
- Gross and net profit margin
- Employee satisfaction – retention/attrition

Sales

- Sales growth
- Leads
- ROI (return on investment)
- LTV (lifetime value of a customer)
- CAC (customer acquisition cost)
- Conversion rate
- Sales ratios (for sales teams)
- Customer service
- Client retention rate
- Customer satisfaction
- Customer service quality and error rates

- Total number of customer interactions
- Team project productivity
- Customer tickets closed (for customer service)
- Time to complete (service)

Staff / Employees

- Voluntary attrition or employee turnover rate
- Number of key hires
- Employee retention
- Employee engagement
- Employee net promoter score (NPS)
- Percentage of managers
- Number of employees and experience (average tenure)
- Performance management (varies from role to role)
- Strategic KPIs for organizational goals or business objective
- Completed reviews and performance appraisals with managers and human resources

Marketing

- Open rate
- CTR – Click through rate (% clicked on a link inside an email)
- Click to open rate (% clicked open email, then clicked link inside it)
- Unsubscribe rate

B2B Marketing

- Cost per lead
- Landing page conversion rates
- Sales pipeline velocity
- Sales close rate

Content Marketing

- Traffic
- Search and keyword ranking
- Time on page
- CTR of internal links
- Bounce rate
- Social shares
- Comments

Social Media Marketing

- Page likes and followers
- Engagement (likes, comments, and shares)
- Reach
- Impressions
- Mentions

Product Marketing

- Free trial and demo sign-ups
- Product usage
- NPS (net promoter score)
- Feature engagement and adoption

PPC (pay-per-click)

- Return on ad spend (ROAS)
- Cost per click (CPC)
- Click through rate (CTR)
- Quality score (Google)

ACKNOWLEDGMENTS

The journey of writing this book, a long-cherished dream of mine, has been a whirlwind of cathartic moments and challenging yet rewarding experiences. However, this dream wouldn't have been realized without the series of unfortunate events and failures that inspired me to persevere and fully embrace the lessons each hurdle brought.

Countless individuals have been a part of this journey in a multitude of ways— some through minor acts of kindness, others with grand gestures of support and faith.

I am indebted to my entrepreneurial parents and grandparents, who instilled in me the courage to dream big, trust my vivid imagination, and believe the world is my oyster. Their teachings shaped me into an independent individual with a burning desire to help others.

My children, Clayton and Cass, are the joy of my life and my greatest teachers, who helped me understand the true meaning of unconditional love. Andy Girgin, Carol Anderson, and Rezan Algun, thank you for supporting me during tough times.

Pam Meier, my oldest friend, you've been the reality check I often needed, offering me insights into myself to keep me grounded. Gayle Lazar, your instrumental support in making my dream come true is unforgettable. The way you showed me the array of gifts and possibilities that lay ahead is invaluable. My heartfelt thanks to Sherri Rothenberg, my unexpected spiritual teacher, and Linda Minghella, my reliable business confidant.

· *Acknowledgments* ·

Eric Olson, thank you for being the best tour guide ever, always making me laugh, and finding ways to disrupt my workaholic routine with memorable beach trips. Jay Stewart, your unwavering optimism, determination, and persistence serve as a constant reminder that success is always within reach. Tammy West, hearing you say I was the best boss you've ever had was profoundly humbling, and it meant the world to me. Adam Bricker, your impeccable timing and thought-provoking questions are always a source of inspiration.

Kim DeBacker-Deveney, I'm grateful for your support of my vision to assist business owners in building a business they love. Denise Farris Scrivener, thank you for pushing me to apply for the Kansas City Business Journal's Women Who Mean Business in 2001. Similarly, Joyce Hayhow, thank you for creating a vast network of talented women business owners that still thrives and inspires.

Over the years of deadlines and distractions, I've unfortunately lost track of many people who have been instrumental in my life. This includes all the brilliant teachers, mentors, and entrepreneurs I've crossed paths with. My gratitude extends to each one of you, including Tom Higley, Branden Holt, John Asseraf, Maria Flynn, Els Thermote, Becky Blades, Lisa Ginter, Tim Murphey, Angela Sharp Hurt, Ray Shank, Tracy Bornman Boedecker, Patrick Sallee, Scott Havens, Aaron Fulk, Tyler Enders, Andrew Coplon, Tony Beck, Mrs. Richardson, Emily Voth, John Dillingham, Christine Spray, Kat McDaniel-Ditch, Heather J. MacKenzie, Cheryl Kellond, Marty Bicknell, Eric Marcoulier, James Taylor, Zhenghua Yang, Dr. Kenneth Bellian, Cathy Caplener, Sumanth Channabasappa, Dr. Michelle Robin, Sheila Seck, Eduord Khoukaz, Susan Desantis Ledyard, Adam Heibert, Morgan Ciani, Matt Fox, Rudy Franco, Jessica Osborn, Greg Maddox, Ron Greenwood, Alan Farris, Diesha Cooper, Steve Tishman, and the many others who've had an impact on my life.

The coaching community (ICF, IOC) has been a significant part of my learning curve, as has the Boulder, Colorado, community's "give first" ethos initiated by Brad Feld and David Cohen. Thanks to my ideal clients, who allowed me to ride along the exciting path to success, and those difficult clients that became a source of deep learning and introspection. Entrepreneurs, small business owners, and CEOs worldwide have my utmost gratitude for their tireless work to better the world.

Finally, I owe a debt of gratitude to Allysen Kerr, who helped me get this book across the finish line and bring my dream to fruition.

RECOMMENDED READING

Delivering Happiness: A Path to Profits, Passion, and Purpose

Author: Tony Hsieh

Publisher: Hachette Book Group, New York, NY

You Are a Badass at Making Money, Master the Mindset of Wealth

Author: Jen Sincero

Publisher: Penguin Books, New York, NY

The Hard Things about Hard Things, Building a Business When There Are No Easy Answers

Author: Ben Horowitz

Publisher: Harper Collins, New York, NY

Radical Candor: Be a Kick-Ass Boss Without Losing Your Humanity

Author: Kim Scott

Publisher: St. Martin's Press, New York, NY

Traction: Get a Grip on Your Business

Author: Gino Wickman

Publisher: BenBella Books, Dallas, TX

Start With Why: How Great Leaders Inspire Everyone to Take Action

Author: Simon Sinek

Publisher: Portfolio Penguin, New York, NY

Clockwork: Design Your Business to Run Itself

Author: Mike Michalowicz

Publisher: Portfolio Penguin, New York, NY

WTF?! (Willing to Fail): How Failure Can Be Your Key to Success

Author: Brian Scudamore

Publisher: Lioncrest Publishing, Carson City, NV

Search Inside Yourself: The Unexpected Path to Achieving Success, Happiness (And World Peace)

Author: Chase-Meng Tan

Publisher: HarperCollins, New York, NY

The Leadership Challenge: How to Make Extraordinary Things Happen in Organizations

Author: James M. Kouzes and Barry Z. Posner

Publisher: Wiley, New York, NY

The 4-Hour Workweek: Escape 9-5, Live Anywhere, and Join the New Rich

Author: Timothy Ferriss

Publisher: Harmony, Chatsworth, CA

ABOUT THE AUTHOR

Pam "PJ" Nurrie is an incurable entrepreneur, successful CEO, Board and Professional Certified Coach, business adviser, public speaker, and author. Pam is passionate about helping startups and mature companies across a broad spectrum of industries tackle challenges to take them from small business owners to the CEO seat.

Pam always dreamed of owning her own company, and her success demonstrates that she was born for business. When she started her company, she was on the brink of bankruptcy with $20,000 in debt, taking a summer break away from her MBA studies. Determined to start a company, she borrowed $5,000 from her parents to buy a pickup truck, tools, and a trailer. She took trade classes at the local vocational school for on-the-job training.

From these humble beginnings, she grew her 100% woman-owned business to fifty employees with multiple millions in annual revenue. After twenty years, she sold her company on a handshake to a venture capitalist.

To further enhance her professional practice of entrepreneurship, Pam returned to school for Evidence-based Coaching. She found that applying the grounded, practical experience she gained in business, with evidence-based theories and models, was a perfect marriage that led her to develop a system for business success.

She has created a curriculum for seminars and workshops attended by over 1,200 people in 56 cities nationwide. She believes that if she can teach someone in one year what it took her twenty years to learn, that's time well spent.

In her free time, Pam enjoys travel and adventure, having lived in Boulder, Kansas City, and Clearwater. She is an avid water sports enthusiast and road cyclist. After years of playing tennis and even going to Nationals, she has taken up pickleball. She enjoys spending time with family and friends, being near the water with sand on her toes, and watching the sun dip below the horizon.

INDEX

A

Accounts receivable 15, 25-26, 53, 138
Affiliates 23
Aflac 177
Alignment 83, 89, 94, 115, 130, 154, 181-182, 195
Artificial Intelligence 176
Asana 156
Assumptions 48-49, 60, 70, 73, 87, 180, 194-196, 198, 204
Awareness 59, 60, 70, 73, 74, 76, 79, 87-88, 90, 97, 153, 155, 180, 185, 193, 195, 196, 199, 206

B

Bayles, David 172
Benchmarking 47, 48, 53, 213
Blanchard, Ken 158
Blaze new trails 204
Blueprint 92, 93, 95
Boyatzis, Richard 67
Bridges, William 184
Brooks Running 177
Buddha 57
Buffett, Warren 35
Bundling 32
Business Assessment xxiii-xxxiv
Business Plan 45, 92, 93

C

Calendar Blocking 202
Capacity 41, 42, 53, 184, 206
ChatGPT 176
Clifton, Don 107
Coaching 68, 70, 124
Competing Commitments 192-194

Confucius 57
Continuous Improvement 59, 61, 173, 174, 175
Cook, Magie 111
Cortisol 136
Cross-selling 24
Csikszentmihalyi, Mihaly 132
Cuddy, Amy 136
Culture 35, 42, 53, 96-98, 106, 109, 111, 115, 116, 126, 170, 172, 206
    keepers 157
    strengths-based 107, 109
    toxic work 79
Customer Relationship Management 22

D

D'Angelo, Anthony J. 189
Dashboard 64, 99, 100
Dave's Killer Bread 177
Delegation 132, 159, 203
Deming, William Edwards 174, 175
Deutschman, Alan 182, 186
Differentiation 97, 170-172
Discounting 28
Down-selling 25
Drop-Shipping 33
Dweck, Carol 196

E

Emotional intelligence 67, 70, 76, 77, 135
Employee engagement 97, 125, 170
Enneagram 122, 123
Excess Inventory 30
Exemplary Leadership 68

F

Farson, Richard E 154
Fields, W.C. 167
Five-Factor Model 122
Fixed mindset 197

G

Gallup 107, 125, 126
Gig economy 35, 43
Gladwell, Malcolm 84
Goals and priorities 36, 44
  setting 200, 201
Goldsmith, Sir James 27, 169
Goleman, Daniel 67
Growth mindset 112, 196, 197, 198

H

Hill, Napoleon 57
Hoops and Hurdles 181-182
Hope Foods 178
Horowitz, Ben 151, 224
Hsieh, Tony 5, 224

I

Ideal Customer 18, 22, 52, 72
IndigoWild 171
Internet of Things 176
Interruptions 71, 144-145, 200-203

J

Jobs, Steve 47, 120, 157
Johari Window 88, 89, 90
Joint Ventures 23-24

K

Kegan, Robert 182, 192
Kouzes, James M. 68, 69, 227
Krishnamurti, Juddu 88

L

Lahey, Lisa Lashkow 192
Larson, Gary 182
Leadership 63, 64, 66, 73, 117, 134
  Democratic 66
  exemplary 68-69
  exercise eight questions 78
  laissez-faire 66
  mastery 75
  middle way 59-61
  poor 137
  primal 67-68
  servant 66
  situational 63, 67, 70, 73
  styles 65, 66, 67, 70
  transformational 66, 70
Lean Management 173
Lencioni, Patrick 157
Lippitt, Dr. Mary 187
Lipton, Bruce 198
Luft, Joseph 88

M

Managing complex change 187
Manufacturing 19, 29, 32, 173
  on-demand 31
Marketing 14, 21, 32, 36, 38-40, 72, 93, 97, 100,
  168, 171, 172, 210

Marshall, Paula 175

Mayo Clinic 197

McKee, Annie 67

Mehrabian, Albert 151

Mezirow, Jack 195

Middle Way, The 57, 58, 206, 207

   principles 59-61

Mindset 73, 146, 182, 185, 195, 196

  fixed 197

  growth 112, 196, 197, 198

Moneyball, the movie 188

Myers-Briggs 122

N

Neural pathways 154, 179, 180

Neuroscience 189

Newberg, Dr. Andrew 153

O

Observe, Assess, and Rework 204

Office Space, the movie 198

Olson, Eric 106, 221

Organizational 60, 71, 217

  design 95

  efficiency 95, 109

  goals 127, 219

  identity ix, 96, 97

Orland, Ted 172

P

Partnerships 24, 26, 53, 60

Pitch deck 93

Planck, Max 179

Posner, Barry Z. 68, 69

Power poses 136

Predictive tools 48

Pricing 18, 27, 28, 30, 48, 53, 168, 169

Primal Leadership 67

Prioritization 200, 202

Procrastination 200, 202

Productivity review 36, 44

Profitability 5, 6, 36, 39, 50, 53, 59, 95, 174, 187

Pro formas 47, 49, 50

Proverbs 153

Purpose-driven companies 176, 178

Q

Quality control xxvi, 32

R

Resistant to change 192

Reticular activating system 188

Return on investment 211, 212, 215

Reynolds, Marcia 124

Road map, business 92, 93, 95

Robin, Michelle 24, 221

Rogers, Carl R. 154

S

Sales Playbook 21

Scudamore, Brian 109, 110

Seasonality 49, 50, 214

Selye, Hans 129

Shark Tank 9, 10

Shaw, Robert Bruce 86

Sinek, Simon 98, 119, 155, 225

Six Sigma 173

Standard operating procedures 43, 162

Strategic partner 36, 45, 53, 93

Strengths Finder 107

Stroop, John Ridley 142

Suppliers 19, 30, 32, 35, 37, 171

T

Taoism 57

Time management 71, 132, 189, 200

Tolle, Eckhart 141, 185

Tracy, Brian xvi

Transformational Learning 195

Truman, Harry S. 63

Tzu, Lao 57

U

Upselling 24

V

Voth, Emily 171, 221

W

Waldman, Mark Robert 153

Wendy's 172

Whack-a-mole exercise 200

Where's the beef 172

Z

Zhou, Luisa xxii

Ziglar, Zig 105

Made in United States
Orlando, FL
16 November 2024

53942763R00147